GOD AT THE CROSSROADS

GOD AT THE CROSSROADS

THE FOUR MOVEMENTS OF

TRANSFORMATIONAL WORSHIP

JEFF PATTON

Abingdon Press
Nashville

GOD AT THE CROSSROADS
THE FOUR MOVEMENTS OF TRANSFORMATIONAL WORSHIP

This book is printed on acid-free paper.

Library of Congress Cataloging-in-Publication Data

Patton, Jeff, 1954-
   God at the crossroads : the four movements of transformational worship / Jeff Patton.
    p. cm.
   Includes bibliographical references.
   ISBN 0-687-49452-4 (binding: perfect-adhesive : alk. paper)
   1. Public worship.   I. Title.

BV15.P38 2005
264—dc22

2005009486

05 06 07 08 09 10 11 12 13 14—10 9 8 7 6 5 4 3 2 1

MANUFACTURED IN THE UNITED STATES OF AMERICA

To my wife, Sandy, for being a living reminder of God's love
To my son, Gregory, for living the adventure with passion
To my daughter, Michelle, for bringing sunshine into our home and my life

CONTENTS

INTRODUCTION

I am sitting in the airport multitasking: observing people, writing, praying, and listening to a worship CD. I am in a transportation hub of a major city. I am in the crossroads of life, where my life, this world, pain, and meaning all merge. In these crossroads, I am intentionally open to an invasion of my space by Someone who knows me and who wants a deeper relationship with me. I am aware that most people are oblivious to so much this wonderful Sunday morning; they are too busy, in a hurry, distracted, trying to catch their flight, unaware of this One.

The sky is deep blue and without a cloud. People are kissing their loved ones, saying sad farewells, walking toward the gate for their plane, going through the endless security. I am listening to an artist sing about heaven and what we can't see but "only imagine."[1] I am aware of four dimensions of life that have converged upon me. The moment is special. I am caught by the intersection of holy things with this lived world and in that intersection I am caught by this Presence, the Divine, the Holy One. Tears begin to form in my eyes, and, while I am not comfortable crying in public, I can sense God has shown up, right here, right now. In these moments I am aware of both the agony and the joy of life, lived right here by this self. I am aware of the hope, the bliss, the sheer joy and delight in living. I am also aware of the pain, abandonment, isolation, and fear that is all around me and within me. These are the crossroads of life, the crossroads of God.

I delight in the crossroads. I am awed that God can invade my reality and in a moment show me real things, real joy. In this moment, God's real presence is manifested in ways I can't see, in a tacit dimension that is barely perceptible to me and seemingly imperceptible to anyone around me. Do they not know that God has come near, shown up as it were? Do I not know that God is near to the many around me? It makes me long that others might know this Presence, and I yearn for ways that I might help them experience God, too. I don't want to argue about religion. I want others to experience what I have just experienced: God came near, touched me, reaffirmed that in this world of chaos and pain, we are loved, we are—I am—never alone. I have had a Divine Intersection right here in the airport—my life, God's life, God's love, God's presence crossed mine in ways I knew were real and powerful. The intersection at the crossroads changes my life again.

If I am going to help others experience this, it seems important to me to know how this Divine Intersection happens. What are the ways we might prepare or develop a capacity for a Divine Intersection? The style of the song doesn't matter. (Randall Thomas's "Alleluia" can do this to me as can Delirious's "God's Romance.") The place is not important. Only two things are necessary: God's willingness to show up and my/our willingness to develop a capacity to be touched by God, on God's terms, for God's purpose. I can't demand this. I can, however, make myself open and perhaps help others to be open to this possibility, this experience. We can create space for a Divine Intersection. We can try to avoid being distracted, stay in the I-Thou-now of the Divine Intersection and try not to greedily hoard the moment.

I can't help wondering how this can be so real here in the airport and so rare in most of the congregations I have worshiped with in the past years. There on Sunday morning when people (me and likely you) most needy of this kind of experience come seeking an encounter (some really do) the congregation is often so busy, so concerned with the urgent that we miss the important. Why else would the announcements be so long, as if this time is really about "us"? Why is there a "sermon" at all? Why do we interrupt the opportunity with things like "offerings" with the lame excuse that this is a way for people to give to God? People can give to God anonymously by placing their gifts or tithes in a box in the back. Why isn't the time dedicated to making space for a Divine Intersection? What are we afraid of?

As I began to wrestle with making worship more relevant and alive, I began to notice that many in the congregation and many pastors I worked with were very uncomfortable with transformational moments in worship. They avoid the crossroads. As I moved from more rigid worship formats, I moved to an awareness of God's presence, even God's desire to be present in our worship. I began to design and lead worship experiences that aimed at making this Divine Intersection a possibility. I have failed more than I have succeeded, but I keep trying because I am convinced that God wants to show up in a transformational way. God created us to "know" God. I believe that is an experiential, emotional knowing as well as an intellectual knowing. The problem is that we aren't often comfortable with those experiences. We have a hard time allowing God to be God. The times when God has shown up were life changing, transformational. People literally left "different." At times they were touched mentally (new ideas); at times they were touched emotionally (felt cared for, felt peace, had weight lifted off their shoulders); at times they were touched physically (pains went away, ill parts of their body felt better and were later confirmed to be better by medical tests); at times people were rebuked, disciplined, trampled to the ground as God made clear the intent and extent of my/their waywardness; at times they were touched in all those ways and especially in the core of their person, in the place where the Divine Intersection is most transformational and real. (Somewhere the mind, body, and soul are joined in this world and impinged upon by negative and holy aspects.)

My flight number was just called. People are hurrying around and I am once again sensing/feeling that God is here. "Where can I flee from your presence," Lord (Ps 139:7 NIV)?

In the pages that follow, I hope to help you cultivate a passion for an experience of God, a space for this Divine Intersection in your life and perhaps in the lives of those with whom you worship. I want to help you experience God by teaching and modeling how to develop a capacity for this Divine Intersection. If this occurs, everything will be different, because you and I can't come into God's presence and not be radically, permanently changed.

It is my hope that at the end of this work you will have a deeper sense of God in your life. It is my prayer that your experience of God will involve your whole heart, mind, body, and spirit and that this experience will be motivational, inspirational, and above all, transformational. To that end, your life will be different, and God's love and presence will be not just intellectual constructs but experientially realized realities in your life. And if I am on target with this notion, not only will your life be different but also others will be changed. The point of these Divine Intersections, as in all of life, is ultimately the fulfillment of God's first priority, what some call purpose: that the world (all people) might know God's love in Jesus.

Someone recently asked me, "What do you want from life?" I would ask you the same question. I have two things I want from life. First, because of the crossroads of God—the Divine Intersection—I want as many people as possible to experience God's presence and unconditional love in Jesus. Second, as Chris Rice has written, at the end of life as we know it here in this lived world, life as we are yet to know it will begin. In that moment, as one reality gives way to another I hope that you can echo these words.

> And with your final heartbeat
> Kiss the world goodbye,
> Go in peace and laugh on Glory's side and
> Fly to Jesus,
> Fly to Jesus,
> Fly to Jesus and live![2]

CHAPTER ONE

THE DIVINE INTERSECTION

In a book on convictional knowing and transformation, Dr. James Loder wrote, "Being human entails environment, self-hood, the possibility of not being, and the possibility of new being. All four dimensions are essential and none of them can be ignored without decisive loss to our understanding of what is essentially human."[1] Transformation or the possibility of new being is possible only at the crossroads or intersection of four dimensions that define life: the lived world, the self, the void, and the holy.

Dr. Loder came to this conclusion during a very traumatic and life-threatening experience. Dr. Loder was helping to change a flat tire on the side of a busy highway when he was critically injured after being hit by another car and pinned beneath the first car.[2] His wife managed to lift the car and drag him out from underneath, injuring her back in the process. In the hospital, as they tended to his wounds and attempted to replace a partially severed thumb, Jim had the doctors and attendants singing hymns. The emergency room was flooded with a presence of God. Many years later Jim was still overwhelmed when he spoke of that experience. The Divine Intersection, the invasion of "the holy" into his life (self, lived world) in the midst of a tragic and critical accident (void) convinced Dr. Loder of the transforming power of God. Dr. Loder sought to understand this transformational power of God even as he believed and received that presence each day. I was fortunate to know Dr. Loder, hear his story frequently, and host him in my home on one occasion. As we shared an evening meal, we paused before we ate. Jim took a deep breath, instantly entering the realm of the Divine Intersection. With tears running down his face we prayed for a simple meal and in that process experienced God's presence in our dining room. Just thinking of this now, a few years after his death, brings tears to my eyes as well as a sense of God's presence. I learned so much in these simple daily encounters.

C. S. Lewis wrote in *A Grief Observed*:

> Meanwhile, where is God?... When you are happy, so happy that you have no sense of needing Him, so happy that you are tempted to feel His claims upon you as an interruption, if you remember yourself and turn to Him with gratitude and praise, you will be—or so it feels—welcomed with open arms. But go to Him when your need is desperate, when all other help is vain, and what do you find? A door slammed in your face, and a sound of bolting and double bolting on the inside. After that, silence. You may as well turn away. The longer you wait, the more emphatic the silence will become.[3]

Does it have to be that way? Can we cultivate a capacity to experience God's presence that will endure even the bitter moments of life? If the only time we feel welcomed by God is when we are happy, perhaps we are deluded. This has not been my experience.

Like Dr. Loder, I, too, was involved in a major automobile accident. I had many injuries and experienced a sense of God's presence that was very peaceful and caring, even in the pain of multiple broken bones and lacerations. When my need was most desperate, I felt God close. In the intensive care unit and later on the main floor of the hospital, I regularly experienced God's love for me. A chaplain in training (Clinical Pastoral Education) came to visit me on the main floor. This person knew me from the seminary where I was studying for an advanced degree. This person looked down at me lying in the bed and asked, "What do you think about God's providence now?" I remember covering my tracheotomy so I could talk and saying what I continue to take with me each day, "God is closer, more real now than ever." The chaplain left without saying another word. There in the midst of life and death, in the pain of an accident, I experienced God's presence, God's intersection with my world, my pain, my very being. And it was transformational. It changed my life.

SO WHAT IS THIS DIVINE INTERSECTION?

The Divine Intersection is the result of convergence of the four basic dimensions of experience, which will produce a transformation of the person. Loder described these dimensions or movements in the following terms.

The Lived World

The environment in which all of life is experienced or lived. "Embodiment in a composed environment is the first essential dimension of being human."[4] It is more than the natural world and is composed of the mental, emotional, and spiritual world. Who hasn't suffered from a broken heart? Who hasn't been hurt by words? Who hasn't sensed a spiritual presence, kind or otherwise? Who hasn't felt the wonder and pain of colliding with the natural world (falling while riding a bike, biting your lip, being bitten by a dog)? Who hasn't seen the wonder of a sunrise, the joy of a rainbow, the power of a waterfall? Who hasn't experienced the joy of a child's laughter or the sorrow of saying good-bye?

The Self

That which pertains to the person: the I, me, myself. You and I are a "self," the embodiment of which (mind, body, spirit) combines in relation to itself and others to make a self. But this is not yet a self. Kierkegaard said, "But what is a self?"[5] The self is not an entity but a relationship entirely unique in relation to its "worlds."[6] Because of the dynamic relationships of the self to itself and to its world, the self, every instant it exists, is in the process of becoming. The self does not actually exist, it is only that which it is to become as it relates to itself, its worlds, and the power that grounds it. Who you are today is not who you were yesterday or last year. You and I are in the constant process of becoming. Each event, each turning of the globe produces more synchronistic meshing of people, paths, and meanings in our lives, which in turn keeps the "self" in a constant process of becoming.

The Void

All those experiences that attempt to rob life of meaning and attempt to steal the sense of purpose, well-being, and meaning. Loder writes, "the implication that nothingness, or negation of being, is ... part of the uniqueness of human being.... The void has many faces ... absence, loss, shame, guilt, hatred, loneliness, and the demonic....Death is the definitive metaphor."[7] Who hasn't been lost? Who hasn't had a relationship end? Who hasn't felt they were being rejected? Who hasn't felt that life might not be worth the living?

The void is anything that would cause us to see life as meaningless. Who hasn't experienced this? A few years ago I was called to visit a young woman, sixteen years old, whose four-month-old baby was found dead in his crib. The young woman was numb with pain and filled with grief. I was asked to do the funeral. I met with her many times, walked with her down a road none of us would want to walk. At the graveside during the final prayer, I heard movement and knew what was happening. The young mother was crawling in the small hole to hold that box, all that was her child, the one she loved, carried, birthed, dreamed about, and now grieved. Life can be full of experiences that seek to destroy you. The void is those kinds of experiences that cause us

4

to lose hope, to turn our backs on life, and to give up living. The number of suicides each year is indicative of the void. The void tears meaning away. What if those of us in the safety of our churches would open our eyes and see the pain around us: divorce, Alzheimer's disease, cancer, drunk drivers killing innocent people, war, earthquakes, famine, tsunamis? Depressed yet?

The Holy

"The manifest Presence of being-itself transforming and restoring human being in a way that is approximated by the imaginative image as it recomposes the 'world' in the course of transformational knowing."[8] It is God's invasion of our life, directly through the Holy Spirit, other people, nature, or any other aspect of creation. God does not allow the void to have the last word. By God's invasion into our world, God transforms the void, makes the lived world meaningful and makes the self valuable. God's Divine Intersection into our lives actually "negates the negation" of the void. Without an invasion of the lived world and the self by the holy the void would destroy all things.

All four areas are necessary for us to experience God. Take one away and you lose the possibility of the Divine Intersection—the experience of the holy in the midst of the lived world, in the experience of the self, negating the void and giving a sense of God's presence with us even in the sorrow.

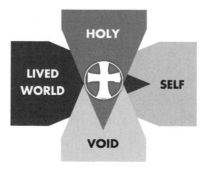

The Divine Intersection occurs in those moments in our lives when *all* four areas converge. It is at the convergence of the four movements that the crossroads of God is apparent, that a Divine Intersection has occurred. In that moment we sense or apprehend that God has drawn near. Often the Divine Intersection does not "change" life. The sorrow remains, death is not reversed, disease is not cured, but at the same time there is an inner change, a transformation of the self that is now empowered to live life in a new way with resources previously unknown. Sometimes the negation is negated. That is, while the external lived world remains the same, new viewpoints/understandings/experiences of God have transformed the event to negate the negative.

God is always ready to invade our lives. We are the obstacle (at least the major one) to the experience of God in our lives. We simply have not thought about the possibility or cultivated the capacity for such an invasion. We spend so much time running from our need, avoiding it however we can. Addictions (work, materialism, gambling, sex, drugs, and alcohol) are real symptoms of a world disconnected from God, dominated by void, and filled with hopelessness. Our avoidance of the four dimensions leads to further dysfunction in every aspect of life. We are short of the fullness of life we could have unless we (self) can embrace the negative experiences (void) in our lives (lived world) and then cultivate a capacity for God (holy) to reach out and touch us (Divine Intersection) in the darkest of days.

So why would anyone want to have a Divine Intersection? And how does each worship event attempt, let alone reach, a point of Divine Intersection? Does the worship experience touch and pay attention to each of the four dimensions? Most do not. Most worship is quite removed from experience of the real world and irrelevant to the issues most people are facing. When in worship was the last time you had someone stand and ask for prayer, talk about their personal needs, ask for help, or in any other way show their humanness? When was the last time you were encouraged to make room for an invasion of God into your world during worship?

TRADITIONAL WORSHIP SERVICE FAILURE

In most traditional services there are times at the beginning of the service to "prepare for worship" such as a prelude or choral number. Many times the noise in the congregation is so loud you can't hear the organ. Many times the organ is played so poorly you can't stand to listen. Then the service begins with a prayer to invite God into our midst (Invocation) followed by a responsive reading. Why do we invite God into God's house as if God were a stranger? Why do we think we need to ask God to show up when "where two or three are gathered in my name, I am there" is what Jesus said (Matt 18:20)? And why do we allow people who have no passion to lead the service and read the lessons, prayers, and announcements with the same emotional joy as Scrooge before his Christmas visitation? When did mediocrity become a virtue?

Every time the service is about to get rolling it's time for another break—announcements for ten or fifteen minutes, the offering (two of them, it's mission Sunday), then more announcements, and the presentation of offerings. Then back to work with wonderful choral or solo music, by instrument or voice. Then another break, standing for a hymn, which has nothing to do with either the scripture about to be read (poorly) or the previous song, or the day, or anything. Then we all settle down for the pastoral prayer. A full ten minutes later (it seemed like thirty), when we have prayed for almost everyone and at the same time almost nothing, it is time for the centerpiece of the morning service: the sermon. I thought God was the centerpiece, but now I am subjected to a twenty-minute speech, which I read on eSermon.com the night before. Okay, the sermon isn't from eSermon. It is much worse. I have sat for more than an hour waiting for a person to finish at least one of the fifteen messages they started that morning. At the conclusion of the sermon, there is a prayer and then another song or hymn. We all stand, sing, yawn, and prepare to leave. Some are angry. Some are bored. Visitors are shaking their heads. Worship, if you can call it that, was not inspirational. The crossroads were avoided. It was pleasant, politically correct, irrelevant, emotionally empty, and a boring waste of time.

CONTEMPORARY WORSHIP SERVICE FAILURE

You arrive to the find the band warming up. The instruments are out of tune, the microphones aren't plugged in, and the band members straggle in with coffee and doughnuts in hand. They are jovial, laughing, and, when they finally get ready to play, they are ten minutes late. The order of the service is predictable, even though they do not have a printed listing of the order. There is a complete lack of expectation here. This week will be like last week. There will be two fast songs; a prayer; one slow song; one solo number; announcements (over ten minutes); an offering with musical overdubbing (a six-year-old violin player doing "twinkle twinkle"); a prayer; a reading from the New Testament; another song; the morning message (again the centerpiece), which is a chat or informal time to "talk with each other" although usually only one person talks; two more songs; and a dismissal. Every week it is some variation of that order. Sometimes the morning message is before the offering, and sometimes it is after the first set of songs. All the negative elements of the traditional scenario are here. This is the same mentality, the same lack of expectation, the same type of neglected unreflective boredom.

Blended worship is a combination of the two above vignettes, except often it is the worst of all worlds. Half of the congregation don't like the hymns. Half don't like the new songs. Most don't like the music quality, and the pastor is usually being pulled by both sides before and after the service, to the point that he or she dreads even showing up and it shows. Visitors, mostly from other congregations, find the attempted union of styles to be undesirable, and most don't return.

Common to all three styles (traditional, contemporary, and blended) is this almost total lack of expectancy that God would or could show up for worship. God is talked to as if God is in another galaxy and the communication device only works when you shout. People have experienced the same lukewarmness for so many weeks that some would frankly faint if God were to make an appearance in any shape or form.

Common to all three styles is a desire, usually by the leadership, to control the events of the morning. Standing on a hose, they wonder why the water does not pour out. They are really more fearful that the hose will fly out of control if they dare remove even one foot. Consequently, these services leave one dry and thirsty for something more, something different, something real.

Common to all three styles is that very few have experienced or been taught how to intentionally make room for an encounter with God. Few have met God at the crossroads. Few have had Divine Intersections. Or if they have had these experiences it was a long time ago, now almost forgotten. Or perhaps they had an experience like this and it frightened them. Or perhaps they just like control more than transformation. To the extent you intentionally make room for an encounter with God, you will begin to experience the Divine Intersection on a more regular basis. Usually this begins on a personal level and then moves to the corporate and congregational level.

The point of paying attention to these matters is missional, that is, the fulfillment of the primary purpose of any Christian community, which is that its members might know Jesus and become disciples. We personally pay attention to these aspects of life not for the goose bumps or "aha" experiences we might have but because we want lives transformed as a vehicle to accomplish the mission of God (which, as I understand it, is some form of helping people encounter, experience, and know Jesus Christ). "All transformational knowing participates in the knowledge of Christ as its norm and paradigm."[9]

You can know if the purpose is fulfilled by the ever widening circle of people whose lives are now different because of these Divine Intersections. As overchurched[10] or pre-Christian people "visit" with you during worship, will they be able to experience what is such a vital and life-transforming encounter? Will the

Divine Intersection be something you not only aim for but also cultivate and reach on a regular basis?

TRADITIONAL SERVICE WITH A DIVINE INTERSECTION

The members of the congregation began arriving an hour before the worship service was to begin. They met for thirty minutes in the sanctuary to pray for the morning service. They pray for the people who will attend. They pray for the organist, the choir, the readers, the pastor, the parking lot greeters, the hospitality desk people, the nursery attendants, the ushers, anyone involved. After thirty minutes some leave to staff those positions, but more have arrived and are already praying for the service in a room right off the main sanctuary. They will stay there the entire time of the service, praying. And what are they praying for? They are praying that God will be honored in the service and that lives will be changed. They know God is there. They know God wants to change lives. They know that they have sixty minutes to touch a life. They know that everything they do is crucial to their mission that all might know Jesus.

The service is to start at 9:30 A.M. but by 9:15 the music fills the sanctuary. The choir and the song leader are prepared for worship. They have spent the last hour at home preparing—praying, reading the Bible passages to be used today (which were printed in last week's bulletin). The acolytes are ready to bring in the light and know that what they are doing is more than symbolic. The Light of the world is here. The adult sponsor prays with them before they enter the room. The songs have been chosen with an eye on two things: God's desire to accomplish the mission and the flow and purpose of this week's entire service, which is directed at changing lives through a direct encounter with God in Jesus Christ in the service. This congregation knows that some are touched by song, others by silence, others by symbol, others by a warm smile, others by prayer, and others by a word spoken in the right time in the right way. The choir processes and the organ swells in great praise. The song is one most know, "Praise to the Lord, the Almighty." It is sung with feeling. The choir in rehearsal last Wednesday practiced all the hymns, as they do every week. While singing it in rehearsal, the choir director, whose mission is to help her choir know Jesus, has explained the hymn's history and, more important, helped the choir to connect the words in their heads with their genuine gratitude in their hearts and to let that gratitude out with their voice as well as their eyes and their smiles.

This congregation has learned that this intentionality, this making room for an experience with God, is what has led this service to grow about 8 percent a year. This congregation now knows that each intentional and purposeful step is crucial. Nothing is attempted without connecting it to four movements of lived world, self, void, and holy. Nothing.

This congregation may or may not know how effective the prayers of the people have been in bringing this all about, but they do know that since they began praying for the worship, the services have been, in a word, *inspirational*. They began noticing that people would be crying while the choir sang or the organ played. So tissue boxes were placed in every pew. They began noticing that when the pastor opened the altar rail for prayer during the singing of the hymn after the offering, more and more people made their way to the altar rail. More tissue boxes. They began noticing that their pastor, once very intellectual and seemingly cold, was now much more open with her emotions, sharing her pains, fears, and hopes in a way that touched lives. Many visitors would comment, "She spoke right to me today."

The entire service was connected by this passion to allow God to appear in whatever ways God wanted. The music, the prayers, even the offering were special times, filled almost to overflowing with God's presence. Everything was an opportunity. Once during the offering, as the pastor was standing at the front of the sanctuary handing out the offering plates, she stopped and, looking out on the congregation, said, "today, no matter what little or large amount you put in this plate, can you, simply by touching the plate, put your life into God's hand for a moment? In that

11

moment, say to God: 'I want to put my life in Your hands.'" As the plate was passed and the organ played, many in the congregation were crying, touched.

When it came time to pray, another young woman came forward and led the congregation in prayer. She asked the people if they might take the hand of the person in the pew with them. She asked them to pray silently for the person on their right, then on their left. She invited any that wanted to pray out loud, to lift up their concerns for others. Many did, just as many did not, and no one was bothered. Then this woman asked us all to be quiet and to listen because God was here and wanted to say something to us. Soon a quiet "amen."

The pastor then rose to read the morning lesson. She then gave a sermon from memory or from a full heart, I wasn't sure. She kept eye contact with us. She told stories that were relational, relevant, full of life—both joy and sadness. She talked about life, sinking boats, disappointments, and new life. She reminded us of God's love and faithfulness to us. She was well-read, bright, clear, prepared, and, even more, convinced God was here to change lives. Her closing story was one she "borrowed" from a great Christian writer. It brought it all together, tied up the entire morning. She spoke of going home and finding a welcome we don't deserve and can barely imagine. It was like a refreshing breeze, and her words brought new life to many young and old followers, as well as to a few visitors who again said, "she was talking right to me today." They will be back.

Before I knew it we were dismissed, and the choir recessed to a great hymn of new life that affirmed God's nearness to God's people.

The pastor had gone to her other duties while a group of caring people were welcoming those who were new at the hospitality desk and others were walking to the prayer room to pray for people or to sit in the lounge to talk. Clearly the ministry of all the believers was an important part of this congregation.

And, yes, this is a real congregation that worships about two hundred fifty in two very different services.

CONTEMPORARY SERVICE WITH A DIVINE INTERSECTION

Same building, same room, except the traditional climate has been augmented by building supplies, a partially erected wall, a drum set, other instruments, microphones, and a screen with announcements being projected. The service will start at 11:00 A.M., but at 10:30, right after most of the people from the first service left, a new crew comes in to pray. While they are praying, three people come in and begin setting up the props and scenery changes. At 10:45 some of those praying move to the side and begin setting up the instruments and music stand and performing sound checks and tunings. Those praying leave for the prayer room, and I notice that many of those going to the prayer room now were in the first service and many of those in the band are part of the group that was praying for the traditional service. These people care for each other and have a passion about their mission. This is exciting.

The band begins playing about five minutes early. It is a song about God's great love called "Fields of Grace."[11] The words are on the screen. The band is good. A young man is leading the band. At 11:00 he turns to the congregation and welcomes us here. He says, "It is great to have you here today. Turn to someone right now and say, 'It's great you are here.'" Before most finish the band is playing again. There is no printed order for this worship. You are not sure what will happen, and I get the feeling the band and leader aren't really sure either. The next song is directed at God.[12] It is more of an affirmation, "Worthy, You Are Worthy."[13] In the middle of the song, while the band is still playing, the leader asks us to stand and close our eyes and imagine we are entering a very special place, a place where God will meet us. Today we will be in God's presence. The song goes on for another minute. Again the leader asks us to keep our eyes closed and to allow the band to play. He then begins talking to God about life, our lives, pain-filled, frustrating, overworked, unfulfilled lives. He asks us to allow God to touch the painful parts of our hearts. The crowd is quiet but the energy is dynamic in the hall. The leader asks us to tell God the things we want to tell him. The band plays

13

on. Someone in the band is weeping. Someone is quietly singing over and over, "You, O Lord, are worthy." Someone steps to the microphone and begins talking. "We are shown a picture of what Heaven might be like. All the believers are gathered around God. Listen to what they say." He begins reading.

> Worthy, O Master! Yes, our God!
> Take the glory! the honor! the power!
> You created it all;
> It was created because you wanted it.
> The slain Lamb is worthy!
> Take the power, the wealth, the wisdom, the
>   strength!
> Take the honor, the glory, the blessing!
> To the One on the Throne! To the Lamb!
> The blessing, the honor, the glory, the strength,
> For age after age after age. (Rev 4:11; 5:12, 13*b*
>   *Message*)

People are weeping. Some have their hands in the air. Some are kneeling. Some are standing. Some are holding each other. Some have moved to the altar rail.

The pastor walks to the front microphone. She asks the band to keep playing. She says, "obviously we need to pray for each other today." She asks an older man to come up to the microphone and lead us in prayer. Soon we are asked to sit. Most of the people who were at the altar rail are in their seats. The pastor pulls a bar stool up to the microphone and begins talking with us. She asks questions about our lives, about our homes, about building relationships. Some talk back to her. Some laugh, nervous talk. Then she backs away and allows four people to do a "skit" about relationships. It is funny, full of double meaning. They are well-practiced and deliver their lines at the right time. At the end of the skit, the pastor is laughing so hard she has to catch her breath. And then she does it—looks us right in the eyes and, with a love and passion I rarely see, says, "your life, my life are full of disappointment and pain. We want relationships that give meaning, and we find ourselves angry with spouse, annoyed at children, frustrated with parents, and, God, you feel so distant it drives us crazy. But then there are moments when we feel at home." She again tells the same story of coming home that she told in the first hour. It fits. "Whatever you have done, whatever you have become, it doesn't matter. Please come home."[14] In the shadows of one side of the sanctuary, a young woman comes forward and sings a song about being finally home. Many are in tears, some are just quiet, eyes closed. The pastor returns, the band is back. We are invited to stay for coffee, prayer, or just stay here for time alone with God. We sing. The band returns to the chorus, "You are worthy, You are worthy."

This congregation may or may not know how effective the prayers of the people have been in bringing this all about, but they do know that since they began praying for the services they have been, in a word, *inspirational*. They began noticing that people would cry while the band sang or played. So tissue boxes were placed in every pew. They began noticing that when the prayer leader prayed, many people found their way to the altar rail for prayer, so people were trained to come up and pray with them. More tissue boxes. They began noticing that their pastor, once very intellectual and seemingly cold, was now much more open with her emotions, sharing her pains, fears, and hopes in a way that touched lives. Many visitors would comment, "She spoke right to me today." And they will be back.

I don't believe this is a matter of style. I'll talk about style and tactics later. The Divine Intersection is the result of the intentional conscious desire of those who plan each worship event to make the hour open to a Divine Intersection, a time and place where God can invade as God wants. To that end, each of the four dimensions deals with issues crucial to that outcome.

Is the worship relevant, does it reflect the world we live in (the lived world)? Do you talk about your life, your town, the world? Do you talk about life and death? Do you talk about pain, frustration, marriages on the rocks, anything real at all?

Is the worship relational, does it engage the various "selves" in ways that cause them to look inward and outward (the self)? Do you lead people deeper, closer to God in that place where God wants to touch and change our lives? Do you open yourself up and allow others to see you, warts and all?

I got word on Saturday night that a dear friend had died. When I was in the accident and healing in the hospital this Greek Orthodox priest visited me every day. We were in the doctoral studies program together and we grew close in those years. I entered worship the next day and knew I could not hide this if I wanted to. All that crap about not talking about yourself in worship is baloney. I walked into worship and turned with tears in my eyes. I talked about this dear friend and then I needed to pray. I could not speak anymore. To my surprise many came to my side that morning to weep and pray with me. Some said to me it was the turning point in their decision to trust me.

Is your worship able to embrace reality, the highs and the lows, the meaning and the lack or disruption of meaning (the void)? Can you hold pain, death, and disappointment in your hand and not drug it out with rationalizations and logic? Can you stand with those who are in pain? Can you hold the hand of the man in pain and not tell him he should not feel this way? Can you hold the woman who has been deserted and not talk about how this will "work out"? Can you just stand there? Can you as a congregation stand with those in pain? Can you touch and embrace the void?

In that environment, are transformational encounters with God experienced on a regular basis (the holy)? What will you do when God shows up? Can you embrace God's love, presence, discipline, joy, and sorrow? Can you be on a constant watch for God to show up and, when God shows up, follow where God leads? This is not an excuse not to prepare or to fly by the seat of your pants. This is rather an intentional, prayerful discernment that God is not bound by your calendar or your list of what is important. Can you begin training your people to respond to God, who wants to change lives more than you and I do? Can you help people gain comfort from knowing that God's presence is always evidenced by transformation?

CHAPTER TWO

PREPARING FOR A
DIVINE INTERSECTION

Some think that worship comes naturally to a person who believes in Jesus Christ. Nothing could be further from the truth or from my experience. Having only attended "worship services" on occasion growing up in a small town in Pennsylvania, I understood that these one-hour obligations were neither fun nor important. It seemed to me that nothing life-changing ever happened. People who couldn't sing mumbled the words and sang off-key. The singing of the congregation was often loud but disconnected from most emotions. People who had very little to say read long excerpts from the most current book they were reading. And that very long period where the pastor told God all the things God needed to know about this group was, in my mind, just a waste of God's time (and mine). As I grew older, my family moved to France and then Germany, where "the church" was in critical decline by the mid and late 1960s. In many of those cities, the tourists outnumbered the faithful 100 to 1 for Sunday worship. The services were even more irrelevant than I could imagine. I fought harder and harder to avoid this emotional, physical, and mental pain. Relatively quickly my mother gave up the fight and let me sleep, which I clearly could do better in my bed than many of the men did in the seats of those sanctuaries.

But worship? I didn't know what that was for years. Even after having a transformational experience in my late teens, I did not know what worship was or how to do it. I lived in at least three worlds at that time. The first and primary world was one of intensity, loud music, and passionate encounters with people who "loved the music" we played: Jimi Hendrix, the Doors, Cream, Iron Butterfly, Bob Dylan, The Beatles, Steppenwolf, Joan Baez, Crosby Stills Nash and Young, Elton John, Billy Joel, Janis Joplin, Led Zeppelin, and Nazz. Even Country Joe and the Fish were passionate. The second world was the one now invaded by a mysterious presence that I only knew as somehow related to God. In that environment we sang upbeat songs about blind men, bridges, troubled waters, sparks that start fires, and a Lord of the dance who was not Irish (while Lord of the dance, we, in fact, did NOT dance). We clapped, sang, laughed, and sometimes were awed by this Presence. On occasions we were invaded by this Presence. The third world was one born of tradition, learned in seminary, forged and hammered into a fit that only works for those willing to learn the language of a culture long gone, never to return. It isn't that traditional forms are worthless, far from it. Those ancient forms can be powerful, full of meaning and purpose if we can only take the time to explore them and adapt them to a generation who never will like "good music." These ancient forms of worship can have new life for those who are willing to do the hard work to uncover their hidden mysteries in the long forgotten symbols and practices (like archaeologists looking for insights from their translations of the Dead Sea Scrolls or art historians probing the meaning of da Vinci's paintings and drawings—what is the knife about in the Last Supper?).

In the first world, the world of rock and roll, there was a search for meaning, answers, and purpose. In the first world there was great music and plenty of passion and emotion. In the first world there was drugs, alcohol, and short-term relationships. There was also death, disease, war, and pain. Just listen to Bob Dylan or Jimi

Hendrix and you can hear the themes of the generation. (A brief listen to current songs such as Evanescence's "Tourniquet" will allow you to hear today's generation's heart cry.[1])

In the second world, the world of the mysterious presence, I learned to hear ancient words in a new light, with new meaning.[2] The ancient message was made accessible to me using elements of the modern world, my world. In this world there was a presence, a wooing, seeking Presence. There was emotion; pain was not ignored; meaning was offered; and relationships were deep. The second world broke down every barrier so that anyone could experience of God.

The third world, the world of "professional religion," seemed to render that Presence inaccessible. Much of what I had experienced in the first world was called "bad" or "sin" here. Much of what I had experienced in the second world was called "emotionalism" and relegated to the realm of the "weird, uneducated, backwoods preacher." Professors and pastors were quick to warn me of the ultimate folly of my experiences in the second world. I only continued in this world because of my encounters with God, what I am now calling Divine Intersections. Let me describe my first Divine Intersection. New Year's Eve (1971) my life was about to change radically. I was not a believer. I was not sure who God was or what it meant to be a "Christian." But I was attracted to some people who had a radiant glow in their eyes. This group had invited me to attend a New Year's Eve party. At midnight we sat in a circle in the living room of a large farmhouse. The people hosting the party brought out a glass of cola and some potato chips, normal food for teens. They said that they "weren't allowed" to use the "real thing," whatever that was. But they talked about One who was broken, and poured out for them, and somehow came back to life. They asked us to take the potato chip and turn to a person beside us and say, "he was broken; all this happened because God loves you." And then we passed the cola around, and we were to say, "this is because God loves you." Even now, thirty years later, I can rarely think of that night without tears. A Presence flooded the room. I didn't have a clue who the Presence was. I didn't know what it meant, but I knew a Presence was there, even as I sense that Presence here right now. I think I worshiped for the first time in my life that night. I was in the presence of the One who did this and who didn't care that it wasn't the "real thing," because this One is the real deal. I, drug dealer, rock and roll guitarist, user of women, rude, crude, foul-mouthed, angry, insecure me, had an encounter I didn't ask for, didn't understand, and couldn't deny. I was moved to thank this Presence, and I wanted the feeling to last. To a large degree it has. In those certain moments when I am desperate, I can go back to that night and once again I am in that Presence who now I know as Jesus. It would be almost six more months before I was willing to surrender even a part of myself to this One. It has been over thirty years and I still am surrendering more parts of myself to him and, to be honest, still struggling to keep parts of myself for myself.

But I began to learn about worship that night. I began to learn that this One is the object, the center, the source of all my life, my passion, my soul. And being in this Presence is more precious to me than breath, food, sex, life. To be honest, I often am lured away by those other things, only to learn time and time again how shallow and unrewarding the temporary is when I compare it to being with the eternal in this Divine Intersection. Since that time, I have learned many lessons about worship, and I continue to learn.

WORSHIP

What I am writing may offend you. Such is not my goal, but the result of speaking of my experience may cause you to question your own practices. I have journeyed for some time on this path, learning to worship in various fashions, in various styles, in various formats. I learned to worship with a very liturgical Anglican (Father John Franklin of New Zealand) to whom I will be forever grateful for his love of hymns, liturgy, the really great thanksgiving and morning prayer. John's order of worship for the Holy Supper complete with extemporary praise and great songs of faith redefined and elevated the communion service for me. I spent years with people we used to call "Jesus People" who were so passionate about Jesus that they would spend hours (literally hours) just singing and giving praise to God. I spent years in mainline congregations doing the one-hour obligation, often filled with strife and contention, where on occasion we would all be transformed by this invasion into our ordinary time by an extraordinary Presence. I spent years doing traditional, blended, contemporary, and cutting-edge worship. I have seen the best of the best, the worst of the worst, and so much in between. I have been moved to tears in all of the above styles and formats, and I have seen what happens when we take our eyes off God and try to copy the world and provide only mediocre entertainment. It isn't pretty, not by a long stretch. In the following paragraphs let me spell out for you some things I am learning about worship.

God Is the "Target"

Many people speak of a "target" for worship. Usually they are talking about a demographic age group or particular lifestyle. Some mistakenly believe that younger people all like the new Christian music. Some think that older Christians hate contemporary music. With these mistaken ideas some congregations will try to "reach" a certain age group with a certain kind of music. While there are success stories and abundant examples of a congregation using one style to reach a certain age group, what will happen as that group ages, has children, and the cycle repeats?

I take a different approach. What if God is the target? What if worship is about this Divine Intersection of the holy invading the human, the infinite incarnate in the lived world of humans? What if worship is not about what we do but about making room for God in our midst? What if worship is about cultivating a place in our lives where God is able to show up, challenge, and comfort us? And what if the best way to make this room is to learn how to sense God's coming near and to yield ourselves to his presence? What if it is all about cultivating a capacity to receive? Consider the following examples in different styles of worship.

Traditional Churches and Divine Intersection

The church was small, fewer than one hundred people in worship, and they were of all ages. This was a very rural part of the Northeast. Their worship was right out of the 1961 Methodist Hymnal (the black one). But their pastor was different. He didn't look different in his robe and stole. But he acted different. First, he stood in the aisle, right there with the people. Second, he was friendly, and he genuinely loved these people, at least most of them. He was real, human. He laughed, cried, and shared his life with these people. They began singing the first hymn, and he led them, although he did not have the best voice. As they were singing, he stopped them after the first verse. It was clear to him that while people were singing they weren't clear about the words or their meaning. The great Luther hymn "A Mighty Fortress Is Our God" was being sung; he said, "like a sand castle." He went on to explain the hymn in common words. He even ventured a guess on what the "one little word shall fell him" might be. Now they sang the third verse with boldness. He ignited a fire in their worship by taking a few moments to explain what they were singing. The entire service changed in mood, attitude, and feelings. Here was a person who had spent time with this Mighty Fortress before worship. Here was a person not content to offer rote phrases without meaning. In my conversation with him following the worship, he said he often stops worship because "we forget so quickly who God is and all that God wants to do in our midst. We come here to worship God, not ourselves, not this building—God. So I make God the center of the worship. I remind them and me often that God IS here and God has an agenda we are to try to find and to live." I could not say it better. Morning worship was about God, and God could do whatever God wanted to do to change lives.

Blended Worship and Divine Intersection

Some say blending worship is the worst of all worlds. But I know a few congregations who have found new life by changing the focus of the worship. Blending the styles didn't seem to hinder them. At a small (under one hundred in worship) rural United Methodist Church in North Central Pennsylvania the worship is clearly a blend. The service starts with hymns, a call to worship, responsive reading, and a prayer of confession with an assurance of pardon. It feels formal, traditional but warm, inviting, and upbeat. God is clearly the target as the service opens with a great hymn of praise like "O Worship the King." The lay speaker who leads the opening each week is careful to keep God the center and the target of worship. There are no vague prayers to a God who might be there. There is conviction that God is with us, right here, right now. "Attitude often determines the altitude," some bright person said, and this congregation has found it is true. The piano player is quite good and the hymns don't go too fast or too slow. The worship is wonderful. Then another person stands to lead in prayer. This person has just returned from a prayer seminar with Terry Teykl, and she is really excited about her ministry to develop a room to pray in this building and to recruit and train ten people to pray.[3] While the area is not heavily populated, except by church buildings on every corner, she knows there are many people near this place who are "dying without knowing God's love, and that is not right." You see that each part of worship is about God. Even the mission to reach out is that others might know God. God is the target. Making room for God is what it is about. Following the prayer time, two young women get up to lead a few songs. These songs are the new worship songs of Delirious[4] and Passion.[5] One plays the piano, the other sings. While we are singing (the words printed in the bulletin), the leader is helping us go "deeper" into God's grace. Transitioning between songs, she talks about her own worship and how God will draw her closer, deeper into God's grace. She invites us to stand, to close our eyes, and to sing words we just sang, only this time to sing them directly to Jesus as if he were standing right in front of us. She asks us to lift our hands. And she breaks off, turns to the pianist asking her to keep playing. Now she turns back to the congregation. She knows that "raising hands" is what "they do," and she makes a funny face. We laugh. She says, "If someone were to rob you and take something from you they might say, 'raise your hands' so they could see what you were doing. That would be frightening. But here in this place I am asking you to surrender too. Only I am asking you to surrender to God, to raise your hands, and, by so doing, to surrender your plan, your day, your troubles, your life to God who is here, waiting for us all to turn our lives over. So now that you know the words, close your eyes and offer God your troubles. Offer God your gifts. Offer God your life. Surrender to God." She resumes singing:

> Lord you have my heart
> And I will search for yours
> Jesus take my life and lead me on.

Some hands go up. She speaks again, not opening her eyes, "If your eyes are closed you won't see anyone watching you." We laugh, a few more hands go up. The mood changes. There were two more songs printed, but we won't get to them today. We will sing "Lord You Have My Heart" for a while, and, as we repeat those lines again and again, they seem to sink down to a deeper place in our souls. Lives are being changed. God the target has targeted us. The beginning hymns all the way to the choruses have paved the way for God to have God's way in this service.

Cutting-edge Worship and Divine Intersection

The band is young, loud. Candles fill the room in this gymnasium hastily converted to a worship hall for this service on Saturday night at 10:00. There are about one hundred people here, most with coffee in their hands. Most are young. Some are obviously feeling no pain. The atmosphere is charged with expectancy. The format of the service will be fast paced, more like MTV than the Hour of Power. There will be video clips, some funny—really funny. The fog machines are working full time. The band, seemingly always present and usually always playing, is once again leading. There isn't much "participatory" singing in the beginning. But after this last movie clip showing a family falling apart, they play a moving song I have heard on the radio. The song, as well as the project images, speak of life, death, suicide, and blood pouring out of our wounds. The young man now projected on the screen talks in short simple sentences. He is their age with spiked hair, earrings, tattoos, but a blazing fire is in his eyes. Tonight God is the target. "God is here, and if you have no hope God is ready to be your hope. If all you have is darkness, God is ready to bring light. If tonight you think it isn't worth going on, listen to Joan." A young woman, dressed mostly in black, is center stage. She tells her story. It is a dark story of hopeless living. The details are painfully real, hitting something in all of us about the truth of life, death, pain, hope, and despair. "I was ready to die. The radio was blaring a song about being lost and pleading to Christ to stop the bleeding and the pain. I put the gun down, and I went for a walk and found myself here, actually out there where you are tonight, and I heard about another possibility. Life. Hope. Meaning. Someone heard me that night. I don't have it all together. But I am alive." (The crowd cheers wildly.) Joan is in tears. There are people throughout the gym praying, crying. Some are looking for someone to talk to. Some just want more coffee. God is here. Lives are being changed. It's midnight and there are still a few people hanging around. Funny, I thought ministry stopped at noon on Sunday. But when God is the target, ministry is ongoing.

In each of these examples, the leaders were sure that God was going to show up. In each of these examples, it isn't the style that mattered. What mattered was the ability of the leaders to help the people make room for God. God is the target, the center of our worship. When we reach that place, I believe we will see more lives changed by God's direct intervention in their lives than by all the manipulative things we do to entertain or seduce a particular generation. Worship is about God—God with us, God ever changing our lives. "I am making everything new" (Rev 21:5 NIV).

Worship Is about the Whole Person

Worship is a matter for the whole person including the heart, what some would call the "seat of emotions." So often our worship is restricted to our heads, thoughts, ideas, propositions. Our willingness to engage our hearts is severely limited. We aren't used to opening ourselves like that. Once, consulting with a large church, I was asked to evaluate their morning worship experiences. All three services were technically well-done, even though they were three different styles (traditional, blended, and contemporary). None of the services touched many people because everything was centered in the head. The message was, "If I only had the right information I could make my life better." Built on European styles and centered in logic, the services were neatly ordered matters with little emotional content. They sang songs (hymns, choruses, new songs) without feeling. "Blessed Assurance" felt more like "kind of a neat idea." "Shout to the Lord" was more like "talk loud about the facts." After the service, the pastor asked me what I thought. I said the services were well-crafted, thematic, thought-out, and executed with precision. The PowerPoint was done well, logical, with fill in the blanks. I said, "They were OK, but I really sensed a lack of emotion, a lack of depth, almost an avoidance of anything which might emotionally touch someone." The pastor, obviously annoyed at my observations, said, "If they want emotion let them attend that independent church. There is plenty of emotion there." He was and is right, and those congregations are growing in almost every city while so many mainline congregations decline year after year. Clearly this church's target was to provide education in three styles. They hit their target. And while there were great ideas, how-tos and strategies for a better life, many I spoke with talked about a lack of emotional depth, a disconnect with the realities of their lives and a frustration that all the great ideas don't often help. Why do we assume that more education will help? Education has never been able to supply humankind with the spiritual needs it craves. Sure, education (the relaying of information from one person who has an opinion, idea, or experience to another person or persons) is vital. Education that is one-sided and does not take in the essential aspects of the four dimensions of life will often become mountains of unusable data. Most people know more about life and the Bible than they can live.

I believe that you can allow life to impart its real emotions to our worship regardless of the style of worship, and technology can help with this. Take the hymn "It Is Well with My Soul," written in 1873 by Horatio G. Spafford. To make a long, powerful story short, Mr. Spafford had lost a son in 1871. Shortly following that tragic accident was the great fire of Chicago where Mr. and Mrs. Spafford lost a fortune in real estate. By 1873, Mr. Spafford had regained his fortune and sent his wife and four daughters to England to work with D. L. Moody, the great evangelist. On the journey to England their ship collided with another and sank in twenty minutes. Mrs. Spafford survived and sent her husband a two-word telegraph: "saved alone." Mr. Spafford took passage on the next ship to England and, it is reported, wrote the words to this song as he was passing over the spot in the Atlantic where his four daughters died.

In traditional services where technology is not used, I simply tell that story and then have the congregation turn in their hymnals and read the second verse. I then share a bit of our common story (lived world) in which Satan buffets us as the Spaffords were buffeted—illness, cancer, bankruptcy, fire, destruction, homelessness, death, grief. Then we read the third verse. "My sin, not in part but the whole." What is it like to know that your failures, intentional or otherwise, are forgiven? What is it to know that God, the great Giver of Life, does not hold one thing against us? "Nailed to the cross, and I bear it no more." Nothing, no sin, nothing can keep us from God—God, who is near, who is here right now. It is well, it is well, Praise the Lord, it IS WELL.

In traditional services where technology is a small part, I will often show a brief segment of the movie *Titanic*.[6] This thirty-second clip shows the large ship sinking and the mothers in the lifeboats watching. One woman exclaims, "O My God!" The sounds of the violins playing on the ship and the screams of the people combine to make "real" the horror Mrs. Spafford and her daughters faced in the mid-Atlantic.

In more blended and contemporary services I do the same introduction and then I show a longer clip, almost a full two minutes. People are dying, diving into the icy water, falling off the bow, tumbling over the propellers. I close with the scene of the mothers in the lifeboats. Then I confess, "I could not have written that song. When I am buffeted, I tend to crack. I tend to scream, yell, and find myself incredibly angry. And here was this guy who wrote these wonderful words about God's great grace in the face of evil that I can't even imagine living through."

It amazes me how many people weep when they see the mothers in the lifeboats watching the ship slowly sink and they think of the words of this song. You see these experiences (void) exist in all our lives, and we do the congregations a disservice by trying to avoid these painful areas.

In a contemporary-style service we sing the same song, only using Audio Adrenaline's version of the song.[7] It is often best if the band can do the number as a solo, asking the congregation to join in the chorus: "It is well, it is well with my soul." From my perspective, if we don't touch the emotions we leave two-thirds of the person untouched.

"The heart of the matter is a matter of the heart," so goes the song.[8] "Where your treasure is, there your heart will be also" and vice versa: where your heart is there is your treasure (Luke 12:34 NIV). If your lived world is off limits, how can God enter? If you put up walls around your life, not allowing anyone, even God, to know of your joys and pains, how can you live? I know people who have experienced incredible pain—the loss of loved ones, children dying tragically, spouses deserting families, financial ruin, and addictions that kill—and somewhere in each of these peoples' lives is the mistaken belief that by walling off the pain they don't have to face it. What really happens when you wall off pain is you also wall off joy. When you turn your emotions off they all seem to hibernate, and you will soon find yourself empty and void of joy, love, and purpose. Congregational leaders often treat each Sunday as if the congregation is "pain free." I look around during worship to see the eyes of the people in the room. Most of the people live lives of "quiet desperation," and I think that most want God to touch that deadness in their lives and revive them. But week after week I see leaders responding like the pastor I mentioned earlier in this chapter: "If they want emotion let them go somewhere else." You know what? That is exactly what they are doing.

I recently visited a rural traditional church in Alabama. To start the worship the pastor called us to come to the altar rail at the beginning of the service to lay all our pains down before we started worship. I was the guest speaker that day and was sitting in the front row with three children who were about ten years old. The one child next to me leaned to his friend and asked, "Are you going up?" She said, "Yes I am going up. What about you?" She asked the young boy on the other side the same question. He answered her, "Yes I am going up." Then the young man next to me looked at me and said, "We are going up, you can go with us if you want." My eyes filled with tears. Here these young people knew something I wish I could teach the adults. Don't just go up and lay your pain down, take someone with you. Take that stranger beside you into your care. He took my hand and led me forward. As the organ played we prayed. We laid our pain at the foot of the cross. It was a Divine Intersection, and it changed me to start the service that way.

I know of a congregation, contemporary in format, which begins its services that way each week. If you have pain, they want you to come forward for prayer. If you need to lay something down before we worship God, come up and lay it down. If you need to be touched with healing from God, come up, they will pray for you.

If your life is off-limits to God, if you can't allow God to break through your walls of defense, how will you ever experience this transformative presence? If you have no passion for God, how will you ever enter into the realm of God's presence, this place where God crosses the absurdity of your life and enters into the joy and sorrow of human existence in powerful, life-transforming ways?

I believe God knows everything I have ever done or ever will do. Do you remember when you were close to God and how you felt? Do you remember the joy of your first communion? Do you remember the wonder of the time you first knew (or knew for the five hundredth time) how much God loves you? Do you remember what you felt at that moment when God was so close you could almost touch God? Well God knew everything you would do right then. God knew you would choose against God in the future and that you would wake one morning to find your life a mess and those you love most terribly hurt and confused. God is still there. God is not surprised. God has not moved. God still loves you, and God's opinion of you has not changed! You can allow God in. God will not harm you. God will not turn you out.

While this book is mostly about meeting God at the cross-roads, it is more precisely about how the four aspects of lived world, self, void, and holy converge to produce transformation in the lives of those who develop the capacity for these Divine Intersections. The larger question here is, *how is transformation brought about?*

Throughout the Bible, people are transformed when, by circumstance or design, their lives are directly confronted by God. For example: Moses turning aside to see the fire that does not consume the bush; Isaiah in the temple; Peter in the boat listening to Jesus preach; and Paul on the road to Damascus. In each encounter the people involved had an encounter with God that simultaneously revealed who God was and revealed their need. Each encounter was a Divine Intersection of the four dimensions of transformation. There was the self (Peter in the boat), the lived world (fishing all night, working hard for a living), and the void (catching nothing). Then, the holy (Jesus orders one more cast and the net is so full of fish it nearly breaks). Peter is undone. Peter (the self) knows who he is. Peter is not fooled, not now, not here. Peter has heard Jesus speak about living (the lived world), and Peter's world is not changed. After Jesus is finished speaking, Peter is ready to go home and get some sleep. He has faced the void all night. Cast after cast with nothing to feed his family, nothing to show for all the work, empty nets (the void). Then Peter responds to Jesus (the holy) and throws the net one last time and the miracle of the fish is clear to Peter. God is near. Only God can do this. And Peter knows he should not be close to God. Fortunately, God ignores all our stupid reasons and shows up to change lives. Peter's response is natural: "Depart from me; for I am a sinful man" (Luke 5:8 KJV). And the joy of God's Divine Intersection is the transformation of lives. Jesus doesn't allow Peter's self-revelation of who Peter is to stop him from showing Peter who God is. Jesus says, "There is nothing to fear. From now on you'll be fishing for men and women" (Luke 5:10 *Message*). You know the rest of the story. Peter is a changed man. One encounter. No offering, no choral response, no benediction. A Divine Intersection occurs whenever you have the four elements combined with a capacity to receive. Peter (self), fishing in the boat (lived world), empty nets (void), and Jesus (holy) equals transformation and purpose, a new life, a new call, empty boats, new friends, new perspectives, new purpose.

It seems to me that we are transformed by God when all four dimensions converge and we have a capacity to receive God's intersection. That is, we have a capacity to receive emotional, spiritual, and intellectual input, which confronts an old way of life and challenges us to a new possibility of life. Change does not occur in isolation from our world, our pain, or ourselves. Change does not occur without God's direct intervention into our existence, a Divine Intersection, which negates false ideas and replaces them with new perspectives, feelings, insights, emotions, and intuitions. We see life, ourselves, all of existence differently with new emotional and intellectual data, and our entire appreciation and experience of life is transformed by this new perspective.

The Shorter Catechism of the Westminster Assembly was clear that the chief end of man "was to know and enjoy God forever."[9] To know God (experientially/emotionally/passionately/ intimately) is to be connected to and linked with God. (Adam knew Eve.) To enjoy God is to be in a relationship characterized by God's presence, not necessarily joy, sorrow, or pain. With the Reformation's (and intellectual rationalism's) emphasis on mind over matter, the place of the heart in worship was replaced by intellectually proper words, formulas, creeds, and now emotionally empty expressions. What matters is what you understand or learn in worship. Thus the spoken word or sermon becomes the focal point of worship.

I am finding that successful efforts to reach pre-Christian people are increasingly holistic, relational, emotionally laden, intellectually stimulating, aesthetically bold, visually pleasing, even aromatic, as every part of human existence is seen as part of the key to having people open their lives.

In the movie *Contact*, the scientist played by Jodie Foster is intellectually agnostic through the majority of the movie. Her reality (lived world), life (self), and pain (void) are all understood from the perspective of an agnostic: if God exists we can't know it and it doesn't matter. Much of our world feels this way. Many of the brightest people in our universities understand her point of view, and they resonate with it. When you ask them, "Do you believe in God?" they tell you they are moral people. And they are! But, the question is not answered. "I don't believe there is data either way. I am a scientist. I would need proof." Toward the end of the movie she has an experience that changes her perspective. I would argue she has something like a Divine Intersection, which convinces her of her worth and the purpose of life, or as she says, "that all of us are important and that we are never, never alone." She asks us to take this all "on faith" with no proof. Well, there is some evidence (twenty-two minutes of static on a tape that was supposedly running for only thirty seconds). That evidence is withheld from Ms. Foster's character. It doesn't matter. Her experience totally transforms her life, her reality, her pain, and her sense of purpose.

The same process seems to happen to all human beings who have Divine Intersections. I use media illustrations like *Contact* to help people around me begin thinking about God and the possibility that they, too, can have an experience like that. In a recent worship experience I led, we used segments of this movie to tell her story. Because it was video-driven (that is, we allowed the movie to tell the story with little interruption), younger people were glued to the screen. Because of the use of appropriate music (from Gregorian chant to John Lennon to Creed to Lee Ann Womack) we engaged a wide range of taste and styles. Because we set the stage in the worship service with songs and a heartfelt two-minute talk about "searching for meaning in the world," people were prepared for an encounter. Because we focused more on emotion and atmosphere, the environment was right for this type of presentation. Because we prayerfully supported the worship, a Presence was sensed as soon as you entered the room. Because we wanted lives to be changed by God's transformational presence, we cultivated awareness of all four elements of a Divine Intersection as part of the first five minutes in worship. A simple two-minute talk about self, the lived world, void, and holy. We asked people to be open to their hearts and their minds.

At the end of the last segment people were crying, smiling, caught up in their own journey with God. Some came up to me after the service with expressions of gratitude. One young man came to me and said, "I came today as a favor to my friends. I hate church. I tried it once a long time ago. I didn't like it. But this, this spoke to me. I'm not sure what I will do with all this. Will this service be like this next week? I want to bring my friends. Can I call you and talk about what I am feeling after I have time to think, and be open in my heart?" I said, "sure," and we set a time.

Prayer Is a Vital Part of Worship

In many worship services, prayer is the domain of one or two people. Of course anyone can pray silently in any worship. What a waste of the time for one person to tell God what God already knows. So try something new. Recently I was teaching a group of "churched people" about prayer. In that I believe modeling is much more effective than lecturing, I simply asked the people to lay their hands on the person in front of or beside them. I then asked them to pray for that person. Many people began praying out loud in what I would consider usually general terms: "God bless this person, keep them, watch over them." I abruptly stopped them and said, "OK, now, ask God how you are to pray for this person." One woman near the back of the room gasped very loudly. I asked the woman who made the loud gasping sound, "What happened to you?" She replied, "I was praying in my usual fashion and you stopped us and asked us to ask God how and what to pray for. As soon as I did that, God spoke to me and told me I should pray for this person in very particular ways about very specific things. It was as if I had just hooked up an information cable and all the data was flowing to me, almost faster than I could take it in. It really surprised me, but it also is so clear to me what you mean. Wow!"

There in that room, away from all the usual aspects of "church," God showed up in a powerful way, changed lives, and taught us to seek God for all things, even how to pray. What if we could help people develop a capacity to worship in ways that allow God to be God, to show up as God desires, invading our lives? What if we would try this on a personal basis first?

Here is a way you can begin to allow God into your life and pain. This week make thirty minutes available for God on Monday, Thursday, and on Sunday before you leave for worship. In those thirty minutes practice ACTS-L.[10]

> A. Adoration—Praising God for who God is. (Holy)
> C. Confession—Admitting who you are and what it is like living your life in this world. (Lived world)
> T. Thanksgiving—Thanking God for what God has done for you. (Self)
> S. Supplication—Asking God for your daily needs. (Void)
>
> I would ask God to come into the pain, expose what needs attention, heal the woundedness, and mend your brokenness. This might occupy most of Thursday's time allotted to prayer. How deep can you go? Perhaps you ought to join with some friends or a small group and explore this together.
> L. Listen—What is God saying to you? Before acting on anything you might have heard, talk it over with a friend, a pastor, your spouse, or a spiritual mentor.

By using this pattern or other prayer patterns, you will begin to develop a deeper capacity to receive from God all that God wants to send your way, including a deeper relationship with God.

What would happen if you would try something like this in your worship? It isn't that hard. This week in the time of the service when you usually pray, do something different. Invite people in the congregation to hold hands (if they want to) with the person beside them. Then ask them to pray for that person. It doesn't matter if they pray out loud or silently. Lead the congregation to pray with an ear toward God. What is God saying to you about praying for this person? How might you pray for him or her in a more specific way? What images or impressions come to mind? After you are finished praying, call the congregation to a few moments of silence. What is God saying to you, to each one worshiping here today? Now I always give this little piece of advice: you may or may not hear or perceive anything. Many never do. If you think you did hear something you need to know that it might be God speaking to you. You also need to know that it might be that the pizza you ate last night was spoiled. It may also just be your own pride speaking. Or it might be from a less than holy source. To keep this practical I encourage everyone who thinks they heard or perceived something to say the following sentences to the person they got this "message" about. "I think I got a message for you. It might be from God. It might be me. It might be worse. So you must promise me you will pray about this and not take it as 'truth' until you confirm this with God and others. OK?"

These are suggestions, and this book is an educative event. But if all I do is convey data and relay facts, you will be unmoved and not helped. Perhaps you will "know more." Perhaps this will only hinder you. I am not that concerned with your end knowledge of my experience, my perspective. I am concerned that you might know God better/more/at all. I believe experiencing God in those moments of Divine Intersection are easier when you develop a capacity and desire to receive all God might have for you. It is as you pay attention to all four aspects of life (lived world, self, void, and holy) that this Divine Intersection can occur.

Developing a Capacity for Divine Intersections Is Essential

To develop a capacity for a Divine Intersection, your worship must be invitational. Everything you do must be welcoming, warm, and open to the new people who are visiting and seeking a deeper meaning from life. Are there people in your parking lot welcoming everyone? Are there people at the doors to your building—yes, all the doors? Are they friendly? I visited a church where Harry was the main greeter at the main entrance. Harry did not like people. He was introverted, shy, and, frankly, not very hygienic; in short, he had body odor. He would not speak to anyone, simply handing each person the order of service without even a smile. Sometimes he would grunt at people. I never saw him look a single person in the eye. When I asked Harry why he was a greeter he said, "It is the only thing they will let me do." Ouch!

Do your ushers like people? Do the people greeting you as you enter the building express joy that you are there or, like Harry, do they just grunt? What is the message you are sending visitors or returning visitors? Many congregations have a time in the service when they greet each other. Most congregations only say hello to those they know. What does your congregation do to make visitors feel welcome?

A few years ago I was going to work with a local congregation as a coach for their new worship service. I arrived on the Sunday before I was to work with them and thought I would just "show up" for all three worship services. I arrived on the property, which had very poor directional signs. I managed to find a parking spot and made my way to the door. As I approached the door the "greeters" saw me coming, set down their bulletins, and walked away. I know what to do in church, so I got my order of service and moved from the hallway into the sanctuary. As I was entering the sanctuary I turned to look back and sure enough the "greeters" had returned to their post and were handing out the order of service to those they obviously knew. The ushers in the sanctuary told me I could sit anywhere I wanted. So I walked up the aisle about seven rows and sat down. Two minutes later a person tapped me on the shoulder. I looked up to see a woman about sixty-five years old. She said to me, "You are sitting in my seat." I said, "I'm sorry. You can sit beside me." She said, "No. I sit right here every week." I said, "Not this week." She sat behind me and loudly sighed the entire service. In this service they had a time to greet one another. At the appointed time in the service when we all stand to greet each other, the people sitting in front of me turned around and reached around me to shake the hand of the woman who was sighing behind me. They never said hello to me. This congregation was attracting all kinds of visitors. But for some reason they just didn't seem to come back. I wonder why?

Another congregation I know was the opposite. This small, rural congregation had people in the parking lot and at all the doors. The ushers were cheerful, helpful, and glad you were there. There were people in the service who came and brought you a fresh-baked loaf of bread. People sat with you, unless you wanted to sit alone, and asked if they could call you that afternoon. Other people made phone contacts and scheduled midweek visits. These people really cared about each visitor. They were invitational.

This attitude was reflected in the worship service. People were welcomed like a guest of honor without ever drawing attention to them. Everyone was included in every event. If you had something to share, you were welcomed to share it. When we prayed, you were welcomed to pray. When we took communion, you were welcomed to partake. No entrance exams, no hassles, no shirt, no shoes, no problem. This congregation was so serious about their mission to help people know Jesus that they discarded the "rules" and focused on people. Before and after the service there was a time for coffee and doughnuts. You could even bring your coffee into the sanctuary. People went looking for visitors and did whatever it took to make them comfortable. Because these people were in prayer for each service, they were attuned to who needed attention and who preferred to be left alone. They didn't badger people. They loved people.

At a large church I worked with in the Midwest, their "after-worship coffee" was a terrible experience. This congregation said, "We are a friendly congregation." Most dying congregations say that. What they mean is they are invitational and friendly to those they know. One Sunday after taking in ten new members they held a "Get Acquainted Fellowship Hour." All the new members went to the fellowship hall where they would greet people and be welcomed into membership. What actually happened was this: Most of the people in worship went home after the service. The fifty people who did stay and made their way to the fellowship hall entered, got their coffee, and sat down with their friends to catch up on the events of the past week. The new members stood around looking very uneasy. One woman I spoke with said I was the only person who spoke with her the entire morning. She was questioning what she had just done. The pastors made their way around the new people, but, honestly, they didn't look very excited either.

So how invitational are you?

Once during worship I saw a young man pacing outside the sanctuary doors. I was in the middle of saying good morning to a few people around me when I caught his eye. I turned the service over to someone else and went out to meet this man. When I saw the fear in his eyes I asked if he was OK. He told me he was invited to attend worship here, but he had never in his life been in a church before. The tie around his neck looked like it was strangling him. I replied that churches can be scary and noticed that the tie was killing him. I invited him to take it off. He looked at me like I was nuts. I took mine off. His eyes lit up, he followed suit. We entered the sanctuary together. That was the last Sunday I wore a tie. He asked me right before the worship started who the pastor was. I said I was. He said, "No way." I said, "Way!" There were some that morning in 1988 who were shocked that I took off my tie. When we had our time to greet people many came up to talk and introduce themselves. As the story got out about the tie, many other men stopped wearing their ties too. Being invitational as a demonstration of the safety of this place is a first step in preparing people to open themselves to a Divine Intersection.

We invite—never demand—people to open themselves up as they grow aware of the four dimensions. We don't need to invite God. God is already here, everywhere. Invocations seem to me to be faithless prayers of the unconvinced. Why would we need to invite God when Jesus said, "For where two or three are gathered in my name, I am there among them" (Matt 18:20)? Just believe this: God is there. Where can you go from God's presence? Do you coach people to be expectant of this reality? Do you, by the way you design and carry out worship, develop this capacity, making room for a Divine Intersection in your worship?

To develop this capacity for a Divine Intersection, our worship must be relational. It must draw us toward God in a relational dynamic, with the I-Thou, the direct face-to-face/breath-to-breath relationship with God before transformation can be experienced. You will need to have people, especially those who lead worship, talk about their personal experience of transformation. Each week you will need ordinary people to stand and talk about the ongoing journey of their personal relationship with God. It is in the ongoing relationship with God and with others that transformation matures. Worship is both a group and an individual dynamic. I would argue that if you don't have regular Divine Intersections alone, you will not have them in a group. You can only go publicly where you have gone privately. While you might have a Divine Intersection alone, it will be more powerful with others, more transformational when experienced by a group.

To develop this capacity, you must be open to a four-dimensional experience. You can't ride the smooth highway of intellect; you must be open to both the intellectual and the experiential. Like in the movie *Contact*, the scientist who can't "intellectually" know God has an "experience" she can't deny, can't turn her back on. I would argue that an experience is always greater than an argument. We can't avoid the four dimensions because to attempt to live in less than the fullness of life would be to shortchange our lives and limit God's participation in our lives.

Does your worship take into account individuals/couples/groups, the self and its experience in life? What are the personal issues, the baggage we carry into every aspect of life? Are you aware of the brutalized, marginalized, despairing people right in your neighborhood? How many in your congregation have thought of suicide this week? How many are celebrating the joy of new birth, anniversaries? How real can you be in your worship?

Does your worship relate to the lived world? Do you take note of the events that happen in the larger world and in the world of your community? Are you aware of the issues that are being faced by the people in worship? Do you know their questions? Do you know their struggles? Have you sat with them and asked them what they are facing? How is God real to that very real struggle?

Does your worship take into account negative, void, meaning-robbing experiences? The accidents, deaths, miscarriages, moral failures, job dismissals, dreams crashing down, and worse are but a fraction of what people face each day. How are you holding those going through such pain? Do you walk with those who suffer?

And have you made room for God to show up? The complexity of our lives is that terrible evil and wonderful blessings abound. Tsunamis and sunrises over calm beautiful oceans are separated by twenty-four hours. Calamity and blessing. God so present in our midst as to make us so clear about life and purpose.

Here are a couple of examples of services open for Divine Intersections in different styles of worship.

The service was very traditional. Formal, robes, sermon centered in the service. The sermon was not exceptional, but it was about having hope in desperate times. Following the sermon a middle-aged woman (self) stood to give a personal story (lived world) with application to the message. She talked about her journey and how hard it has been for her and her husband. And she started to cry. The husband rose and stood by her side. The pastor came down and likewise stood there. They didn't rescue her, they loved her. She continued talking about giving up hope, drinking herself numb, and wandering off to another man for a different relationship and winding up twice as empty (void). But then God showed up (holy) in this "other man," who loved her and told her to go home to her husband and work it out. I remember her closing words, "The pain comes for a reason. The longer you run from the pain [void] the further you run from God. Embrace the pain, face it, and invite God into your pain." Following her words the pastor invited couples to the front for prayer. Only a few came forward. In the months that followed more and more found their way to that couple's small group, new ministries developed for married couples. Today couples flock to the front to pray each week.

The service was contemporary and in a rut. Three fast songs, two slow, announcements, message, good-bye and gone. In the middle of the second fast song the worship leader stopped us all. He (self) knew the band was faking it. He stopped playing. He aired the dirty laundry. The band was fighting (lived world), feelings were hurt, people were leaving the band, and some were leaving the congregation (void). And he knew it was mostly his fault. The song he was playing was "The Happy Song," but he was very unhappy. He couldn't sing, couldn't lead. He set down the guitar and stood at the microphone. He confessed his anger at God, at band members, and at life. And then he asked for help. Most in the crowd were stunned and seemed paralyzed. For a moment no one moved. Then a young girl, barely fifteen years old, stood up, walked to the front, and knelt at his feet. She began to pray quietly. Soon others were gathered. Lives were healed that day. God had shown up (holy), changed the order of the worship, changed the mess, changed a few lives. Relationships were restored. Hurt feelings were addressed. A Divine Intersection occurred, transformation was the result.

In both services there was a moment when it was clear that the direction of the worship was changing. In both services it was clear God was doing something different in the lives of those involved. In both services there was resistance to following the new direction. In both services the congregations were taught to be open to God showing up and doing a new and different thing. In both services the leadership could have shut it all down with one word, one joke, one of those "not this" kind of looks. In both services the leaders were comfortable following God's leading. In both examples you can see all four elements of a Divine Intersection.

When I was seventeen and searching for understanding of this mysterious Divine Intersection in my life, I was with a group in the hills of West Virginia. One evening we were asked to go outside and be quiet for twenty minutes. In that time we were to listen. Listen for God. The preceding hour had been a laughing, crying, wonderful time of knowing other people, seeing life in a new perspective, facing the negatives in life, and developing a capacity for experiencing a Divine Intersection, although this group would not have called it that. In my twenty minutes, I was quiet and aware of this Presence, pushing me, demanding of me my time, my life. I was aware that while I did not know what this Presence was, I was at once trustful and terrified, and in that moment I was changed and transformed. Well to be honest, the transformation was beginning. The last thirty-one years have been a roller coaster of a ride. In my freshman year at college I had a philosophy professor who was raised Jewish, converted to Christianity, became an atheist, and then became a philosophy professor. He was brilliant, challenging, and very logical. When he discovered that some of us were Christians, the Introduction to Philosophy class became the philosophy of why there isn't a God. For the next twelve weeks it was battle after battle. It energized me. I discovered Kierkegaard, who not only helped me think but also showed me one way Christians can think about the world in very deep and challenging ways. I also discovered many other bright men and women who helped me think about God in a new way. Yet one thing remained. No matter how strong the good Dr.'s arguments against God were (and some were great), I had this experiential encounter with this Presence who pursued me and who would not let me go. In one of the last classes, the professor demanded to know how I could keep holding to this ridiculous idea about life and God. I simply said to him, "You have an argument. I have an ongoing experience. Obviously the experience is greater than argument, than words, than even logic." He threw the eraser at me and stomped out of class, and, for the next few moments, the class and I talked about my experience (or what I would now call a Divine Intersection).

Just a cursory look into heaven in Revelation 4 offers us a glimpse of worship that is both head and heart. People, animals, and other created things are passionate, bowing down, shouting, day and night saying:

> Holy, holy, holy
> Is God our Master, Sovereign-Strong,
> THE WAS, THE IS, THE COMING.
> Worthy, O Master! Yes, our God!
> Take the glory! the honor! the power!
> You created it all;
> It was created because you wanted it.
> To the One on the Throne! To the Lamb!
> The blessing, the honor, the glory, the strength,
> For age after age after age. (Rev 4:8*b*, 11, 13*b*
> *Message*)

Not much there is not emotional, packed, full, overflowing. How many times has our worship resembled that? Yeah, I know, let that other congregation do that. We are going to worship "decently and in order" (1 Cor 14:40). That is, the chosen will worship as if they are frozen.

Worship Must Be Visual and Sensual

In the movie *The Matrix Reloaded*, there is a great worship scene. Yes, the preacher has his time (Morpheus speaking to the crowd). But the people are ecstatic, emotional, and full of passion, and the worship is sensual. Could you imagine worship being that passionate? Why are we so concerned with order? What is decent and in order? Is elders falling down before the throne decent? Is shouting, singing, dancing naked like David before the Ark, weeping, and raising hands decent?

Visual: Worship has been visual, a pageant if you will, for ages. In this pre-Christian world of the twenty-first century more visual aspects will help our worship. Candles, pictures, stained glass windows are the visuals of the last era. They still work. Use them. Don't shy away from visual aspects. Decorate the worship hall. Take the theme of the morning and use it. Some of the visual aspects transfer across style lines. And yes it is a stretch for some, but if you don't stretch you will grow stiff, rigid, and closed to the transforming presence of God.

One Sunday before Easter the theme was all the junk in our lives. The worship team transformed the front of the sanctuary into a junkyard. It was quite a sight. It was a visual portrayal of a hidden and secret junkyard in our minds and hearts. It worked in all three services: traditional, blended, and contemporary. There were more in the traditional service that liked it than in the contemporary and more in the blended service that disliked it. But it worked.

Sensual: That is involving the senses. Every service ought to touch all the senses. This is hard work but it can be done. Again the style of the service doesn't matter. I was at a very formal funeral and in the middle of the service the aroma of chocolate filled the service. The deceased was a guy who loved chocolate. The priest leading the service stopped in the middle of the liturgy and commented on the aroma, attributing it to the cooks in the basement. At the meal following the worship we were all surprised that there was "no chocolate anything" baking in the building. Why can't we think intentionally about that in our worship? In a service about returning "home" one worship team brought an oven to the sanctuary and baked chocolate chip cookies and brownies. The room filled with the aroma. It reminded people of "home" as a place of sweet aroma and good things to eat. As part of the service hot cookies were passed out (yes, they baked a bunch more in the basement), and we were told to go and share a cookie and invite people "home."

For a Good Friday service I gave out old-fashioned cut nails as a take-home reminder of what occurred on that day. It seemed more fitting than a gold cross. Gold crosses are for Easter. Nails are for Good Friday.

In a service on "What to Do When Your Boat Sinks," I pass out LifeSavers. We decorate the entire worship hall with items from boats: oars, life preservers, captains' hats, sails, anchors, and throwable life rings. Then I pass out two wintergreen LifeSavers. This is both visual and sensual. You get to see it, feel it, touch it, have it, and, yes, eat it. Invite me to your church for the rest of the story. I might even take you "sparking."[11]

These examples work in any style of worship. In one congregation I did the LifeSavers in only the blended and contemporary services. The next week there were many complaints about neglecting the traditional service. That taught me that you can adapt most illustrations to most styles. You will never make everyone happy. That is not the point. The point is to create an environment in which God can show up and transform lives through a Divine Intersection.

Presence-Based Worship

Terry Teykl, friend and nationally known prayer evangelist, just released a book, *The Presence Based Church*.[12] What I am calling the Divine Intersection, Terry has called Presence-based church. "While other churches are seeking more people, the Presence-based church is seeking more of God."[13] Terry writes, "Here's the hard truth—in many churches today, the Presence of God is absent. He doesn't sign the attendance book on Sunday and he's on the inactive roll.... The Presence of God is not necessarily welcome or essential for this kind of institution to operate."[14]

What a sad commentary on the church. It is also why I write these words. I want the presence of God, experienced in what I call a Divine Intersection, to be a regularly occurring transforming event in the worship of every congregation in this world. I want each worship experience to be so transformational that unchurched, pre-Christian people will leave worship and know that their lives will never be the same. I want Christian people who have attended worship week after week, year after year to walk from their sanctuaries this week transformed by a Presence that will not let them go and that will pull together all four dimensions of their lives into a transforming event that will pursue them for the remainder of their lives. I don't care if the pastors are upset, if they must forsake the "sermon" for another week or stop taking offerings. All these things are a distant second to the possibility that God will show up in our worship and change lives from the inside out.

DESIGNING WORSHIP FOR DIVINE INTERSECTION: WHOLEHEARTED WORSHIP

eveloping a capacity or making room for God is not simple or easy, nor does it occur on a demand basis. The
object of the worship is God, not the feelings or the
human experience of God's presence. Sometimes we make those
feelings or experiential components "god" and forget totally
about God. The Prophets are full of stories where the outside of
the bowl is clean and the inside filled with crud. Religious people have this great tendency to make the experience more
important than the God who gave the experience. So we keep
going back to the retreat center, the campground, the spot where
God showed up twenty-five years ago. Each year we are more dis-
appointed that God did not do what occurred that first year.
God, on the other hand, is out to know us and to fulfill the
intent of God's heart, namely to have a dynamic life-giving relationship with God's creatures (John 10:10b). To that end God
will not be tricked into any dog and pony show. God is already

there, at your elbow, but our lack of honesty often hinders God. I believe that God desires these Divine Intersections more than we do.

I was talking to a woman recently who told me of how lonely she (self) was in youth and how painful (void) her memories are of those days (lived world). As she was talking she remembered herself lying on her bed, crying, "just like I did almost every day." I didn't say much, asking her to remember those days and going to that room where she spent her teen years crying, alone. I prayed. I silently asked that God would intervene. I had no clue what was going to happen, if anything. She gasped and then said, "Jesus just appeared in the room [holy]. He is sitting down with us, me as an adult and the teenage me. He is saying something. I don't understand the words. I think he is singing." She began to cry. Later she e-mailed me. She wrote the words she was hearing as Jesus sang to her. She thought it was some kind of blessing, but as she focused on the words it was clear Jesus was singing, "I am the God who sees, who saw." It freed her from pain (void) and transformed much of her pain and anger to know Jesus saw, was there, and is with her now. Perhaps if we say less in worship, direct less, Jesus will show up in transformational ways that touch the deep pain (void) in our lives. That experience is worth one million times what my words are worth.

Once in worship we did a rendition of Lee Ann Womack's song "I Hope You Dance."[1] Before we played the song I asked people to be open to an experience with God that might be different. I don't try to lead people to have experiences that are forced or forged. Instead, I want them to be open to the invasion of God into their lives in ways that are God-directed and transformational to them. We began the song and at the same time projected images on the screen. About halfway through the song a woman in the middle of the congregation began crying, staring at the screen. Then more people were crying. One young man knelt, then another. Over and around the first woman there was this, well, "light" that appeared to shine down on her. There were fluorescent lights in the room, but this light was more like a spotlight, more direct and, while bright, was yellow not white, and the light was warm. Others around her noticed, yet they were seemingly untouched, peaceful but not very emotional at all. At the end of the song we were just quiet for a few moments having a sense that God was not finished with us. Then the woman spoke about seeing Jesus coming to her, touching her, and giving her a deep sense of assurance about her life, her current difficulties, and her life's purpose. I did not know that this person was considering becoming a full-time pastor. I did not know her at all. But there in that experience her call was affirmed, her life was affirmed, her difficulties were carried, and she left with new direction and purpose.

If we can get out of the way, preparing ourselves for an intervention, it amazes me how many times God shows up.

At a large ecumenical gathering of pastors and leaders I was given the joy of leading worship. In that venue I have worked with others to develop multisensory experiences of worship.[2] For this event we used a work we call "Do You Know Him?" The service begins with Gregorian chant while images of the creation of the universe are projected on the screen. The songs move from Gregorian chant to John Lennon to Creed to Matt Redman singing a version of "The Wonderful Cross." The video of the song is a blending of the hymn "When I Survey the Wondrous Cross" with a modern chorus or refrain. The video was filmed at an event called *Passion: OneDay Live*. The song is long, more than fourteen minutes. In the middle of the song, two young men carry a wooden cross to the front of the outdoor worship arena. As they erect this cross, people from the crowd, at first simply watching, now begin to walk and then run to the cross. These young men and women begin to throw themselves at the foot of the cross. Tears streaming from their faces, they reflect the passion and reality of lives being touched by God. More and more people come forward, wanting to touch the cross. The worship leaders are ready to end the song. You can tell it has gone on too long, but God is doing something more important than what fits our time frames. The worship team begins to sing again, repeating the chorus:

> O the wonderful cross, O the wonderful cross
> Bids me come and die and find that I may truly
>   live.
> O the wonderful cross, O the wonderful cross
> All who gather here by grace draw near and
>   bless Your name.[3]

More come, more want to be close to this cross. In the worship venue I was leading, there were many who "wanted" to come up to the front of the hall, many who were quietly sitting, wiping tears from their eyes, many who were surprised that God could use a video and speak to their own lives about God's love, purpose, and direction. It took intentionality. I prepared them during the worship time for a Divine Intersection. I helped them risk being open to the possibility that God was searching for them. I invited them to open their hearts and minds to God's presence. I led them step-by-step from doubt to possibility to actuality to heartfelt response. Among the people who spoke to me later, one woman said, "It was all I could do to stay in my seat. I wanted to run to the screen and throw myself, my life, my heart at the foot of that cross. I have never done anything like that. My church has never made God's presence so clear to me. I can't wait to take this back to my congregation and help them develop worship like this."

THE MISDIRECTION OF TARGETING

It is a very human mistake to worship the experience of God's presence instead of God. We like that sense of God near, we like the way it makes us feel. Those of us who are more emotional like the tears, the special touch, the way we hear God speak to our hearts. Those of us less emotional aren't that thrilled with the feelings but may like the effects on others when God touches them (like a full altar rail, many decisions for Christ, larger checks in the offering plate). Sadly, we all tend to worship the experience. Many congregations have ways to begin or close worship that at one point were quite moving and meaningful. At one time people experienced God's presence in the little song before prayer or in the closing song. But now, thirty years later, the song makes little sense, it is sung with little meaning, and no one remembers why we do it.

Contemporary worship styles are equally prone to this phenomenon, which is why many contemporary worship services start with three peppy songs, move to slower, emotional songs, share a prayer or a teaching, and then have a very emotional song at the end. It worked once, or maybe still works occasionally. While many of these congregations are proud that they aren't bound by bulletins or orders of worship, the truth is they don't need one because each week is the same and everyone has the service memorized. In more emotional congregations you don't need an order of service but you can set your watch to the time when Sister AlwaysLoud will stand and speak a "word" from the Lord! Or the time when Brother Brightsuit will begin dancing like a wild man and then fall over.

There has been (and most likely will continue to be) this trend to offer worship that is "targeted" toward a particular demographic group. There has been much written about how to do baby boomer or baby buster or Generations X, Y, or Z worship. I would dare say I think these days are just about over. I don't hear of such tactics in third-world or other countries. Worship styles might be highly varied and contextual. I would argue that without developing a capacity for Divine Intersections, no "style" of worship will be transformational. And why would you want to do that?

SPIRITUAL INCLINATIONS

Another mistake we make is that our hearts are not right when we come to worship. And worship is a matter of the heart more than any other part of our lives. Where is your heart with Jesus right now? You may know a great deal about Jesus, but do you really know Jesus?[4] We come to worship tired, strung out, frustrated, needy. We haven't spent the time we need with God all week, and now it is Sunday and we aren't ready to be in God's presence. Some of us are on a constant run from God, as if when God catches us we would have to die or something. We want a predictable, tame God. What did Mrs. Beaver say about Aslan? "Safe ... course he isn't safe. But he's good."[5]

A very successful pastor of a large church had a problem at home. His family could never make it to worship on time. Week after week his wife was late for worship, late getting to the band, late getting the children to children's church. When she did appear she was obviously stressed out, tired, irritable, unspiritual. So he rearranged his schedule so he could take a few weeks to "help his family get to worship on time." I mean, what could be hard about getting three children up and to worship on time? The first week he was up two hours ahead of time, had the children up, showered, dressed, and then, just as he got everyone in the car, the youngest child threw up breakfast. The two teens were not about to ride in that car, and mom took the young one in to clean and change. After fighting with the two teens and making numerous trips into the house to help speed his wife along, they all arrived at worship angry, exasperated, tired, and late. Two more weeks of his "help" and things weren't any better at all. But he began to get a feel of what it was like to come to worship ready to kill someone.

Most people who attend worship on a Sunday morning may not be as exasperated as my friend, but neither are they ready to worship. They come after a week of fighting traffic, the schools, the children, and sometimes each other. They come empty, with hearts full of questions, minds filled with thoughts that might be anything but pure. They come with a sense of duty and a hope that perhaps they will find something that will stir them emotionally and challenge them mentally. And I would argue most come with one last hope to gain something that will make a difference in their lives. Sadly most leave untouched!

ENTERTAINMENT WORSHIP

In the past there has been much written and said about "entertainment" worship.[6] But what has struck me is that, in most of these services that work, it isn't just the tactic of style that has been impressive or transformative. It has been the intentional effort of the worship team (no matter the style) to offer worship that touches people in the four dimensions. Pure entertainment worship is just about over, as is pure traditional, pure blended, pure contemporary, and pure cutting-edge worship. Apart from the deliberate intention of creating an environment for a trans-formational Divine Intersection, worship is often boring, or worse, irrelevant! How can we take one of the most wonderful and exciting aspects of life and make it so dull that some fall asleep during the worship hour? What we usually get is the worst of all worlds: the emotionality of Scottish Presbyterians and the intellectualism of a serpent handler.

What I am proposing is what some people call "wholehearted worship," something that involves the totality of what it means to be a human being. Why does our worship not reflect the exu-berance of David, dancing and worshiping before the ark? Why is our worship so centered in "be still and know"? I want it both ways. I want to worship with my mind—I still read Kierkegaard, Augustine, Aquinas, Luther, Wesley, Packer, and McGrath. I still listen to Bach and Mozart. But I also like Yaconelli, Lucado, Compolo, MacArthur, and Warren, and I listen to Audio Adrenaline "cranked to 11" and my houseplants are fine! I want to use all that God has created in me, including my body, to pres-ent to him a living, active sacrifice for all God has done for me, for all that God will do, and most important, for who God is. I want to sing, dance, think, move, sit, kneel, lie, be quiet, shout, and whisper faster, slower, in comfort and in pain, in excitement and in dread, in assurance and in doubt, in fear and in trembling. I want to live this life, these very short three score and ten, with all the gusto I can give let alone grab. I want to worship God with all I am, all I have.

So I worship frequently. I intentionally set aside about ninety minutes to worship. Each day the format varies. Sometimes I lis-ten to music, sometimes I play my guitar or piano. Sometimes I am quiet, meditative, watching the sun rise or set in awe. Sometimes I am on knees, sometimes standing at the window singing at the top of my lungs. Sometimes I am singing ancient arias, opera, bluegrass, country and western, swing, praise music, or Dan Hicks. What I have learned is that if I don't worship daily, I can't lead worship well. You must stay in touch in order to help others get touched. It is in these personal times that I have discovered the new song that has led me to a place where God has shown up, touched my life, and made me different. I also ask members of any worship team to tell me about their personal worship times. I find that if your worship team (design, band, tech, drama, and so on) isn't engaged in personal worship each day (or at least three times a week), they will not be able to lead worship in a public forum.[7]

THE MISDIRECTION OF "MAGIC STYLES"

In the recent past there have been many types of worship styles. Of course there is traditional worship that is as varied as the many denominations across the world. What might be very traditional to an Episcopalian might be seen as very contemporary by a Greek Orthodox worshiper. And what might be very traditional to a Southern Baptist might look very contemporary to the Episcopalian. So even though we toss out terms like *traditional* or *contemporary*, by now it is common knowledge that even within any given denominational or nondenominational heritage there are multiple meanings to those words.

The attempt to make the gospel of Jesus Christ relevant to the unchurched, pre-Christian masses is not a new idea. Songwriters have taken familiar tunes and added words reflective of their Christian experience for centuries. Great debates have taken place about using instrumentation in worship. Great conflicts were created by people who tried to introduce the organ into worship (and more recently drums, although timpani in classical music was considered OK).

Today there are all kinds of styles for worship: traditional, contemporary, blended, cutting-edge, rap, jazz, southern, country, casual, swing, Taizé,[8] emergent,[9] and many more. My point is not to attempt to define these various styles. I simply point out that in this postmodern world, there are as many styles as there are preferences or microcultures. Unfortunately most of these styles might attract people initially, but there is little to grow them into contagious followers of Jesus. Why does this happen? I believe it is because the majority of congregations designing worship start by misdirecting both target and use of styles.

I know of church starts and plants that were begun in the sincere desire to reach more people with the wonderful good news of God's love and grace in Jesus Christ. Some have gathered a great band, and they have practiced long and hard. They have prayed long and hard for God to bless their efforts. They have advertised well, spending thousands of dollars to get the word out. At the first service there were three or four hundred people in attendance. The next week the worship attendance number dropped by half. The week after that there were one hundred people, mostly people from other churches looking for a new place. Within two months there were sixty-five regular worshipers. Visitors continued to drop by, but fewer and fewer were coming each week. I have asked church planters about this and most have said to me this is common. Yet I know other church plants that have started with twenty-five people in the basement of a private home and in five years there are thirty-five hundred people in worship at the local high school. Church planters I know tell me this is unusual. I have the same question about both experiences. What makes the difference?

I believe the desire to reach people by accommodating to style changes is just as erroneous as the inflexible nature of those who have not accommodated any style changes. Those who accommodate have often been so focused on reaching people they have missed the point of worship. Those who have not accommodated have focused so hard on what used to work that they, too, have forgotten the main point of worship. It is a misdirection of energy to focus on styles too long. Any style is a possible venue for a Divine Intersection. If God is not a "respecter of persons" what makes us think God is a "respecter" of our worship styles?

When people motivate themselves to go to worship on any given day, they are exerting tremendous energy against a much easier and more comfortable option of staying home, having coffee, and playing with the kids. So they make the effort, they get up, they find their way to the location, and they enter the building with a mix of fear and hope. What will this service be like? How will I be accepted? Will this bore my children? Will this bore me? Will anything scary happen? Will this freak out my children? Will I leave challenged or transformed when the service is over? Some say those questions are answered in the first ten minutes a person steps on the grounds of the facility. By twenty minutes in either you have them or they are just waiting to leave. If you are at all serious about reaching those who visit with you, you must take this seriously. The feel of the worship, not just its style or look, is a crucial aspect.

Frankly, from my perspective, if God is allowed to show up in a transformational way I don't care about the songs, the style, the looks, or the theological stance. If people are genuine, have a deep faith in God, are excited about having strangers in their midst, and have been praying for a Divine Intersection for their lives and in the lives of those who are worshiping here, then the presence of God in this worship will change me, transform me, and bring me back. If, on the other hand, the people are cold, demonstrate apathy toward God, aren't excited about visitors, and aren't praying, the coldness in the air turns me away at the door.

My wife and I were traveling and, as is our custom, stopped on Sunday morning to worship in the town we were in. We entered the front door and almost turned around. The place was drab, cold, bleak, dimly lit, and dusty. The men at the door were unfriendly and reluctantly handed us a worship flyer. We sat near the front of the church and no one sat in front of us. Of the fifty people in worship that day no one was under sixty years old. The hymns were sung without feeling. The responsive readings were read without feeling. The message was about beavers and being industrious. God, Jesus, and the Holy Spirit were never mentioned in readings or message. At the end of the service people began greeting each other. No one talked to us. As we were leaving, a woman spoke loud enough for us to hear: "Who are they?" Not to worry. We are from out of town and even if we come back to this town we won't stop here.

The organist of a large Lutheran church told me he had written a piece for the worship service I would be attending. He was reflecting on the goodness of God, and this music began to flow out of him. At the traditional service he played this piece as a transitional piece between the Old Testament lesson and the New Testament lesson. As he began to play, the atmosphere in the room changed. I closed my eyes and began to soak in the wonders of God's presence. This was a Divine Intersection. God's presence was very powerful and transformational. Tears began to flow down my face. I was hearing God speaking to my heart. My experience was short-lived as the couple behind me began talking. She said to him, "Do you want hot dogs, or should we call in pizza for lunch?" He said, "We had pizza last night, and I hate hot dogs." On it went, oblivious to the reality that God was here, present, willing to invade our lives. Even the pastors were missing it. They were so busy preparing communion or finding the next passage that they didn't have time to notice that God was creating a Divine Intersection. As I looked around the room there were others who were likewise wiping tears from their eyes. There were many others who had cultivated an ability to experience God's presence and were open for this Divine Intersection. Sadly there were many more who were talking about lunch.

I was visiting friends in a large Midwest town and traveled downtown to a new church that recently began offering worship in a new style. The jazz service was just beginning. The band was having a great time. The music was so loud you couldn't hear yourself speak. There were no greeters, no ushers, no signs, no way to get yourself around. Fortunately it wasn't crowded either. The coffee and doughnuts table was obvious, and, sadly, the doughnuts were all taken and the coffee thermos was empty. The service was chaotic. The band would play, but how do you sing with jazz? Most sat and listened. There was a drama in the middle of the service, but you couldn't hear the spoken lines because the microphones kept cutting out. There were some visuals in the room. They were mostly modern art of indescribable form in mostly black and red colors. There was no order of service, nothing that told you anything about this project, these people, how to get more information, or if there was anyone who might want to know you. Somewhere in the middle of the service the one leader asked all the new people to stand. I did not stand. No one did. The guy knew there were people here for the first time and so he asked again and again. Still no one stood. Someone else came to the center and read something from a modern poet. I got lost in that. Then there was a commentary on the poem. The band came back, the music got loud, and people began walking out. I left feeling that no one had a clue what they were trying to do. They were being very cutting-edge, trying to attract the avant-garde of the upscale urbanites. They might attract people once, but why would anyone come back? After the service I asked their leadership about the number of people who returned. The leadership said they didn't try to track that. I asked what was their target, and they told me the demographic group they were hoping to be "relevant with." I asked to what end they were attempting this. With shock in their eyes at how I "didn't get it," they told me I would "not understand." This was not about changing lives. This was about providing a new way to do church. It was new. I didn't see how it could work disconnected from anything transformational. Two years later the project was reduced to a few band members and one of the founding leaders. Soon afterward the service was canceled.

If worship does not embrace all four components of existence (self, lived world, void, and holy) it will not be transformational, it will not promote new life. If the worship is not transformational, why waste time and energy doing it? If people are not coached, mentored, and taught how to develop a capacity for Divine Intersections, their lives will not be changed.

Styles of worship are simply tactics. What might be indigenous here might not be there. And while indigenous is vital, it too is merely a tactic. What is transformational is cultivating a capacity to receive a direct invasion of our lives as we are encountered in the four dimensions of life, in a transforming Divine Intersection.

The alternative to the misdirection of targeting and the misdirection of styles is the appropriate strategic map (not plan).[10] By focusing on the four dimensions of life and by cultivating an openness to an invasion by God into that life, worship moves from targets and styles to transformation. The path to this place is relatively simple but certainly not easy.

DNA

Developing a capacity for these Divine Intersections begins with the person who has had one of these experiences and who knows how helpful these experiences are in living for Jesus Christ. Within that person is an inner understanding about encountering God's presence. This experience has changed them from the inside out. They cannot talk about God without talking about how they have encountered God and how it has changed them. They have had their spiritual chromosomes changed. They have a new spiritual DNA in them.

This new DNA seeks to reproduce itself in others. Imagine if we could inject a substance in a person and it would alter their DNA so that diabetes or cancer would no longer be able to affect them. What if we could change the spiritual DNA in people so that they would eagerly seek transformational experiences and want to promote those experiences in our worship?

Changing worship begins with changing the DNA of existing congregations (especially if they are not used to God's presence or Divine Intersections in their lives.) Every worshiping community needs to be very clear about its DNA. Our spiritual DNA is composed of purpose, principles, and people.[11]

> Purpose is a clear, simple statement of intent that identifies and binds the community together as worthy of pursuit. It is more than what we want to accomplish. It is an unambiguous expression of that which people jointly wish to become. It should speak to them so powerfully that all can say with

conviction, "If *we* could achieve that, *my* life would have meaning." *Making a profit is not a purpose.*[12]

By principle I mean a behavioral aspiration of the community, a clear, unambiguous statement of a fundamental belief about how the whole and all the parts intend to conduct themselves in pursuit of the purpose. A principle is a precept against which all structures, decisions, actions, and results will be judged. A principle *always* has high ethical and moral content. It never *prescribes* structure or behavior; it only *describes* them.[13]

I would add that our faith conviction also plays a part in our principles. As people of faith, our convictions inform and determine our behavior.

Purpose and principles are, in my opinion, the place to start. If you aren't clear on your spiritual DNA, your purpose and your principles, you won't get far before you are derailed, sidetracked, defeated, and confused.[14] "If you don't know where you are going or why, any road will get you there."

A part of the new DNA, built on a clear purpose and clear principles, is to know the target. The target is God, not people. The Divine Intersection is a Presence-based, transformational worship that always has God as the target. God is the target, and as we plan for worship that flows from our DNA, the purpose will be confirmed and enhanced as our worship makes the Divine Intersection the point of our worship. Whether it was Moses on the mountain, Isaiah in the temple, James and John at the transfiguration, Peter in the boat with Jesus, Paul on the road to Damascus, the disciples on the road to Emmaus, the Corinthians in worship, my life on the hillside of West Virginia, or your life right now, transformation through the Divine Intersection is the aim; God is the target; and contagious, changed lives in Jesus are the hoped for outcomes and goals.

TEAMS

To reach this goal on a regular basis, worship can no longer be the domain of one person. This will take a team.[15] The teams will need to be primarily composed of people who own the DNA and who have gifts/talents for the particular area they are responsible for in the overall design and implementation of worship. Each congregation will have to determine what teams to develop and how extensively to develop them by its size, number of interested people, and available funding. Smaller congregations may have two major teams involving fourteen people. Many of the sub-teams I will describe in the following paragraphs may not be feasible due to the lack of people or funding. Middle-sized congregations may have many of the main teams and fewer sub-teams. Larger congregations may break down these teams into more extensive subteams. Each congregation is unique and the object is not to be like your neighbor's church. The object is to be the congregation God is calling you to be, to provide your congregation an opportunity to hear the gospel in a language they will understand, that they might experience God's transforming presence.

What is a team? Components of a team usually include a coach, players, and support people, which often include people willing to serve or cheer the team on. In the following lists of teams, my experience leads me to a chaordic arrangement for each team.[16] In a chaordic team, each team member is valued, appreciated, and respected for their unique perspective and input. Hierarchy and team are not compatible in my opinion. While the coach of the team may have responsibility for accountability of the team, the coach does not have the final say, the entire team does. Certainly the input from the coach is vital and will be respected, but the coach is often not on the field playing and can be out of touch with the lived world of the players. I know of congregations that are truly team led. The coach (pastor) may have vital input, but these wise coaches also know that the team collectively is wiser, more informed, and better able to discern the direction than any one individual. There may be a few occasions when a coach will push for a direction, but the more the coach disregards the team the less creative the team will be, the less trust will exist between the team members, and the effectiveness of the team will proportionally decline. Coaches with control issues will find teams perplexing, and they will need a change in their spiritual DNA if their teams are to prosper.

For teams to maximize their effectiveness they will need to practice brutal but fair honesty. Learning to speak the truth in love (Ephesians 4) will be crucial. Clear self-defined "I" statements will be necessary. If we can't talk to each other honestly and with love perhaps we should go home. The same would be true of speaking the truth from anger or with intent to harm. Equally dangerous is overlooking disagreement in a vain effort to have peace at any cost. So often the ego strength of team members is an issue. So many pastors/coaches cause teams to be ineffective by trying to stifle ideas they don't agree with or by maintaining a "one up" hierarchical position. One congregation I know of has a team of twelve who, if they were to agree, could ask the lead pastor to step down and the lead pastor would gladly step down for the cause of Christ. These people trust each other explicitly. This pastor has been quoted as saying, "My team of twelve has the authority to replace me whenever it becomes necessary."[17]

The following are teams I find necessary to develop: Prayer, Worship Design, Music, Drama, Multimedia, and Hospitality. The list is in the order I would develop them.

Prayer

Developing prayer ministries is the first major task. Prayer ministries undergird the entire effort by developing teams who regularly pray for the worship services, including praying for all the people having responsibility in those worship services. These teams would also be praying for an increased capacity of the congregation to embrace the four dimensions of life that Divine Intersections might occur more frequently in the life of the worshiping community. Developing prayer teams will take intentional effort. To begin these teams I would suggest you hold a weekend seminar with Terry Teykl or one of his staff. As Terry walks your congregation through the basic and advanced principles of prayer, you will find that a passion will awaken in some of your people. This passion is usually twofold: First, these people will pray more themselves. Second, they will pray that others will likewise be motivated to pray. Prayer will become a part of the principles that compose the spiritual DNA of your congregation. As those with increased passion to pray gain momentum and numbers they will develop a special room in your building for prayer. As prayer becomes more intentional, there will be special seasons of prayer in the church year. Each worship service will be a time for prayer. In some "emergent congregations" there are prayer centers open all during worship, places you can enter and people there will pray for you.[18]

In one congregation we tried this experiment: we hosted a prayer seminar weekend with as many congregations in the area as we could convince to come. After the event we developed a prayer room in the building where many met regularly for prayer. During the course of the weekend it was suggested that if we want our services to be an opportunity for transformation, what I am calling a Divine Intersection, we would be helped to have a team in the prayer room praying for the services as they were being conducted. One of our leaders recruited other like-minded people to gather in the prayer room to pray for worship services as they were happening. Immediately the climate in the worship changed for the better. The atmosphere seemed full of God's presence. People could sense a difference. The music sounded better. The sermon had a greater effect. The choir sang with increased passion and more new people found their way to the worship services. I believe this team is the most overlooked and underdeveloped aspect in a congregation's quest to be transformational.

Worship Design

Theme development and coordination of the weekly services would be the primary responsibilities. This team would prayerfully discern the direction the congregation is being called to and would attempt to propel the congregation to greater faithfulness and effectiveness. Theme development would include subjects to be addressed, issues to be covered, and creative ways to address those subjects and issues. After praying together, the first agenda of this team's meeting would be to brainstorm and reflect on the prayerful discernment of each team member. Special emphasis would be placed on how the purpose or mission of the congregation would be reached in each service. After brainstorming for the first part of the time together, the team would turn their attention to this week's services and theme. Much of the actual legwork for this week's service will fall to the subteams that develop out of the needs of the worship design team. I have developed six subteams to cover the work needed to design, implement, and carry out transformational worship. The main worship team would have one representative from each of the six subteams. In this model, the worship design team is the primary "fractal."[19] While the lead or teaching pastor should be a part of this team, this, like all teams, would have a level playing floor. As in all true teams, this team would passionately hold the DNA and, as "iron sharpens iron," would propel each member to greater effectiveness for the sake of the mission. The final part of the team's weekly meeting would be to evaluate the previous week's worship experience. These evaluations must include a realistic accounting of the service's ability to accomplish its purpose. If the service does not help the congregation accomplish its purpose, changes must be implemented, even if the majority of the people "like" the worship "just like it is." We can never forget that the point of all we do is to accomplish the purpose for which God created and called us.

Music

This team's responsibility is to find or compose suitable music for each week's theme. Again the primary task is to enhance the capacity for a Divine Intersection for each participant. This team would be responsible for the songs and music that are a major factor in the receptivity of a Divine Intersection. The music, whether from the 1500s or recently composed in alternative sounds, is a major aspect in this process.

The music team would be composed of four people. One of the people, most likely the worship leader, would have the dual role of responsibility for leading worship and serving as the representative to the worship design team. Each congregation can set up the various parts of this team as they need. What I have found helpful, if you have the personnel, is to have the following four people on this team: sound and tech setup person, instrument team leader, guest or special music coordinator, and the worship leader, who would be the person to work with the vocalists, mentor the entire band/ensemble, lead rehearsals, mentor others to become worship leaders, and, of course, lead worship.

As leader of the musical ensemble and directly engaged with all the music of worship, the worship leader is a pivotal person. Ideally, they should be people of deep faith who are regularly exploring musical styles and able to incorporate many different styles into the worship services. Perhaps the most important quality of a worship leader is his or her personal and corporate experience of being in and leading others to experience a Divine Intersection. Worship leaders, at least all the good ones I have known and learned from, have a clear sense of who they are (self), have no delusions about their situation (lived world), have gone through their own share of pain and disappointment (void), and have encountered God (holy) on numerous occasions. These leaders have an inner attention to God's presence. They, like our fathers and mothers in the wilderness, have an uncanny gift to sense the presence of God. They watch for the pillar of fire by night and the cloud by day. They seem to know when God is drawing near. They know how important it is to stop running when God manifests in our worship. I have often caught them quietly praying, discerning, asking, "What is it, God, that you want to do in our midst right now?" On a personal basis, effective worship leaders are frequently in worship, privately and corporately. A worship leader taught me, "You can only go publicly where you have been privately."[20]

There is a great song by Matt Redman called "Seeing You."

This is a time for seeing and singing
This is a time for breathing You in
And breathing out Your praise
Our hearts respond to Your revelation
All you are showing, all we have seen
Commands a life of praise
No one can sing of things they have not seen
God, open our eyes towards a greater glimpse
The glory of You, the glory of You
God, open our eyes towards a greater glimpse
Worship starts with seeing You
Worship starts with seeing You
Our hearts respond to Your revelation
Worship starts with seeing You
Worship starts with seeing You
Our hearts respond to Your revelation[21]

"No one can sing of things they have not seen." If you haven't seen these things, odds are against you leading anyone there. How often do you spend time in the Divine Intersection? How regularly do you build in a capacity to receive a Divine Intersection?

I recently interviewed three people for a "worship leader" position at a local mainline congregation. All were people from the surrounding community and not people who worshiped in this congregation. All were bright, gifted, talented people. All had passion for Jesus Christ. Yet one stuck out as the clear front-runner. The pastor and I did the interview together, and, when we spoke afterward, it was clear to him as well. The one had a "deep spiritual experience of being in God's presence on a regular basis and a passion to take others there." I could not have agreed more. It was the combination of hearing the person talk about going deeper into God's presence and the delight in the eyes when talking about leading other people into a direct encounter with God in Christ that won me over. I am not sure what this congregation or this person will do, but I know who I would hire in a moment.[22]

Drama

This team, like all teams, would be composed of at least four people. There are at least four areas that a drama team would need to address: actor recruitment and rehearsal, play or script development, props, and a director/coordinator. I would think the director would be the person who would be a part of the main worship design team. As the director participates with the main worship team in theme determination, the director would return to the drama team to brainstorm; research themes; recruit and train actors; and find, design, and arrange props. This team would determine what short skits, short one-act plays, readings, dialogues, or full-blown plays would contribute to the week's theme.

The right drama, the right word at the right time, can be the necessary ingredient to the experience of God's presence. Rehearsals and coaching of the actors is essential. You can't grab a few people a few hours before the service, give them pages of notes to read, and think you have a drama team.

I have seen dramas, skits, and readings in all types of services done well. At a very traditional church I witnessed a moving one-person interpretation of the Gospel of Mark. I have seen a three-person skit in a blended worship service. I have seen very serious issues addressed, and I have seen great humor. I have used ideas I have heard on Broadway, off Broadway, community theater, TV, and public radio.[23]

Contemporary congregations who use drama well are Willow Creek, Ginghamsburg, and Community Church of Joy in Arizona. I have found myself worshiping there on occasions and have often sensed God's presence through well-done drama. I have personally written some short skits using models I saw at one of these congregations or on TV.

Multimedia

This is an increasingly important team in the creation of worship that will move people toward Divine Intersections.[24] The multimedia team may have many people, as their tasks are varied and their labor is intensive. Who said computers will make our lives easier? A team coordinator will be necessary to keep direction and production deadlines moving. The major areas of responsibility are: photography and video (many congregations are developing their own "clips"[25]); the discovery and use of existing media (movies, predesigned video, DVD clips, nature scenes); sound tracks and effects; and the training and use of presentation software. Each of these areas will require a team of people. In doing people-on-the-street interviews, a popular multimedia application of both late night TV and many congregations, you will need at least three people for the street work: camera operator, interviewer/spokesperson, and producer (someone to get releases signed and to keep the crowd away). Back at the main facilities there will be a team who will take the material from various sources and edit it for use during the services. This is very labor intensive and will require someone with extensive knowledge and skill in editing, formatting, and delivery. Some of these people will necessarily be present at each service to deal with the inevitable glitches as well as the project management and display in the worship service.

Smaller congregations may feel overwhelmed here, but they need not be. A smaller congregation needs only a few people who have a passion for this type of ministry. In these smaller congregations one good computer and one person who can edit is all you need. Of course, you wouldn't want to use this type of project each week. Perhaps once a month will suffice. On this smaller scale, perhaps the worship team doesn't have a computer, let alone anyone who can edit video or graphics. Perhaps all you have is a television and DVD or VHS player. In this congregation, a thirty-second clip from a movie might be all you need. I have often seen a segment of a movie that communicates a truth better than I could with words alone. I could list almost every motion picture I have ever seen and show a place in that picture that I think would be relevant to communicate a thought or idea that will be transformational.

In a series on the Ten Commandments, I had the opportunity to preach on adultery. This congregation had a television and VHS player. After a skit in which we highlighted the term *adultery* we moved to a passage of scripture in Proverbs (ch. 7), which spoke about how such a decision will ruin a life, or in older language "cost you your soul."[26] We then showed ninety seconds of a movie in which a man is learning that his adulterous affair has resulted in a pregnancy, and the woman wants to birth the child and raise it, assuming the man would be "happy." Instead the man says, "you don't understand, this will ruin our lives." The scene is real, it is life, it is powerful and conveys the ancient truth of Proverbs with a dynamic effect. This segment highlighted the man (self), his family and job (lived world), the possible ruination of life through betrayal and mistrust (void). This set the stage for the introduction of the holy in our worship as God can redeem even those life events that seem to bring ruin to our lived world and to our selves.

The day of a few boring PowerPoint slides with words on them is just about over. Instead thematic, visually appealing motion pictures on which words and ideas are displayed or in which a story is told seem to be growing.

While attending a medium-sized congregation in the Midwest with a traditional worship service, I was surprised to see video clips and PowerPoint slides being projected on the wall to the right of the pulpit. The slides were colorful, well-designed, and, ten years ago, would have been extraordinary. The slides were well-done—all the words were spelled right. The backgrounds were mostly nature photos, beautiful but dull. Most of the slides, and most of the service, was not connected to the theme of the morning. To their credit someone had placed a "prop" on the pulpit that was very helpful to the theme. This prop could have been used more centrally. Instead, the service was chopped up, separate from the theme, and gave the impression that we plug the message into an already existing format. Everything must service the purpose or mission of the congregation and each service is helped by hanging everything—the hymns, call, responsive reading and scripture, props, and PowerPoint slides—to the theme. At midpoint in the service there was an offering taken with an organ offertory. While the organ was played excellently, the static nature picture with the word *offering* across the center of the screen was tacky and a poor use of the medium. Instead, the team could consult with the organist about the "offertory" and, based on the type of music and what the music was intending to convey, could develop a motion picture that would be more engaging and tie the worship to the four elements necessary for Divine Intersection. On weeks when time and energy don't permit such development, a still photo alone or a blank screen would work so that the congregation could allow God to "show up" as the organist leads the congregation in worship.

I can hear the smaller congregation saying, "We don't have the time or resources to do this." And you might be right. I would argue that you have some high school students who are already doing these things and might be looking for an avenue to use their gifts in God's service. You may have a few who have the passion but aren't sure where to go from there. Contact some of the people I have mentioned here. Go to their Web sites and see when they are offering training events. Attend worship at some of the larger congregations who use multimedia on a weekly basis and ask them questions that will help you get started on this project. This is not an issue about size. This is about passion and calling.

By the middle of the week the multimedia team will have all the projects well under way and ready for presentation before the worship design team. It is here that some projects are tabled and others are promoted. Learn the lesson of the pack rat. Don't throw anything away. Keep every project. You might not use it now, but you might use it in a month.

Tech: A Subteam of Multimedia

The responsibility of this team would be lighting, sound, and video projection that occurs during the worship services. This would include the look and feel of the room, the atmosphere: the set design and props being used. There isn't much worse than a dynamic worship service ruined by terrible tech: screaming speakers, bad batteries in the microphones, lost cables, burnt out projection lamps, locked-up computers, misdirected spotlights, missing props, or worse. And, yes, it can get worse.

It is the responsibility of the tech team to do a rehearsal the day before the service and to be ready to go at least one hour before the service. A run-through rehearsal for every tech aspect of the worship is crucial. Are the batteries fresh? Are the microphones and monitors on and working? Is the projector on and in focus? Are the speakers on? Have they been checked and tested? I can't tell you how many times the tech items were great in the office or ran fine at home and now at the worship center nothing will work.

One Sunday the worship team had prepared a tremendous video-driven experience designed with the Divine Intersection in mind. The main video guy[27] and I were working hard to develop this theme and put it all together. The finished product worked wonderfully on his home computer. Sunday morning we were all ready to go. The team was excited, the bands and choirs had all done their parts. For whatever reason, the projector would not receive or show the image from the computer. Three services later, all without the whizbang video, the task was accomplished. We created the atmosphere in the room, the songs were right, the video crashed and burned, the Divine Intersection occurred. We simply knew what to say and when to get out of the way. In recent months I have used that video with dramatic results. The tactics can get in the way. So in this both/and world, be careful. Thou shall not love thy tactics more than thy God!

Hospitality

Welcoming and first-touch ministries would be included in this team. From the time visitors set foot on the property until they drive off, there should be a plan as to what kind of reception they receive. This reception, next to prayer, might be the major contributor to the capacity of a person to be vulnerable to a Divine Intersection.

First-touch ministries are the front line for making the visitor comfortable and safe in worship. Most people who will visit with your congregation this Sunday have been to a worship service before. Almost 60 percent of the people in America have had some experience with worship services. So these people come with an experience of worship, and usually it is not a very welcoming one. Most congregations think they are friendly, and, truthfully, they are; they are friendly to the people they know. The visitor, the stranger, is often not welcomed. What is the "first touch" visitors have with your congregation?

At a very rural congregation in the Northeast, teams of people stand ready each Sunday morning to greet, welcome, and guide visitors around their small but beautiful congregation. These teams know that most visitors will decide whether to return or not in the first three minutes. That is not a lot of time. How do you help people to have a favorable experience in the first three minutes? These teams, after an introduction, ask visitors if they want a tour. Would they like to know where the important rooms are? Nursery and bathrooms are the two rooms most new people with children check out first. Are these rooms spotless? Does the nursery staff seem warm and friendly? Is the nursery a place where I would want my child to spend an hour? If little Suzie or Johnny leaves the nursery and tells mom, "I didn't like that person," odds are that family won't be back. If the bathroom has an odor and is dirty, they won't be back. How important is it for your congregation to make the effort to attract and keep visitors?

Other first-touch ministries occur in the worship center, around the coffee table, in the hallways to and from the parking lot. How many people have shirts that identify them as "Guides" of your congregation? How many of your people are thrilled with new people? How many see that new person as a person of sacred worth who has come to this service on the outside chance that they will have a life-changing encounter? A story I heard years ago highlights this for me.

John loaded the gun and set it down on the kitchen table.[28] He looked around the house, now empty of the sounds of his children. The marriage had been rocky, and his wife had left and taken the children with her. To make matters worse he had been out of work for almost a month and the prospects looked bleak. Bills were mounting. Hope was dying. A friend had dropped by and invited him to worship at a congregation across town. A long drive but perhaps it might help. If this didn't help, he knew what the loaded gun would do. If he came home from this worship with no hope, no reason to live, he would do what he had to do. John parked his car where the man in the parking lot pointed him. John got out of the car and the man, obviously bothered by a sore leg, walked to him. With difficulty speaking Bill introduced himself to John. John was amazed that Bill would be putting so much effort into parking cars and meeting people. Bill pointed John to the main door and said that someone would meet him there. As John turned to walk away, Bill helped the next car find a spot. John entered the worship center and was met by friendly people who helped him find his way to the coffee table and to a seat in the worship area. After the worship, Bill was there again, helping people exit the parking lot. Bill engaged John and asked for his phone number, which Bill wrote down on a pad he kept in his front pocket. Bill was friendly with John and asked if it would be OK to call him sometime. John mumbled yes, got into his car, and drove home. It was a slow drive. Nothing he had heard this morning helped much. The worship didn't touch him. He parked the car and made his way into the house, walked over to the kitchen table, and picked up the gun. And the phone rang. He almost didn't answer it. He picked up the phone. It was Bill who with difficult speech said, "Are you OK? When you left you seemed so sad. Is there anything I can do?" John was overwhelmed. As he poured out his story, Bill asked if he could come over and see him.

I was in that congregation the morning John told his story. Now three years later he and Bill park cars for the church. John has survived a divorce, sees his children regularly, and attends worship each week. He has learned from Bill how to look for and recognize people who are desperate. He has learned from Bill how to care. He has learned from Bill that Jesus will never leave him, never desert him. The small group John now leads is made up of men who are coming through divorce. John (self) and his reality (lived world) were facing more pain, separation, and loss (void) than he could stand. Bill came and brought hope and God (holy) into John's life with transforming power. It wasn't the worship or the band or the great multimedia that made a difference. It was one person who was using his gifts to serve God that a transformation might occur, that John might have a Divine Intersection.

It is the responsibility of each team to recruit and equip others to serve on these teams. Each team should know which gifts and talents are necessary for their team. What personality traits will work best in a given team? Do you understand that creative people tend to be persnickety about doing what they do well? Can you make room for excellence with attitude?

It would be the understanding of all the team leaders that mentoring others to do the task is more important than doing the tasks themselves. Mentoring is a complex set of behaviors. First you recruit and equip those who are gifted. Then you lead them, teach them, and grow together as a team. Spending time together as a team is essential, not just on the job but relaxing at the coffee shop or in a home is crucial. This is the best way to communicate and transplant your congregation's DNA. More will be "caught" than "taught" in these teams. Eventually, as the team members learn the needed skill set, you encourage them to attempt things on their own while you stand near to help if necessary. As they become more efficient you can allow them to continue the mentoring process by giving them the responsibility of training new people. That will free the team leader to do more oversight of the emerging teams and to recruit more people for the existing team.

If the team leader does not have the DNA, it will become apparent quickly. Jesus' admonition that you can tell a tree by its fruit is applicable here. If the DNA is nonhierarchical and your team has power struggles, something is amiss. If the DNA is prayer, honesty, and small groups and your team members don't regularly pray, hide their real thoughts and feelings, and don't participate in any small groups, you have a problem. And usually the problem will be evident in the team leader's life. Our teams will learn what we live. They will be drawn to it as a moth is to a flame. When that doesn't happen there is an issue that will need to be addressed or the DNA will be compromised and decline is inevitable.

What about the smaller congregations, those with fewer than fifty in worship? Where would you find all of the people required for these teams? Perhaps you could do something incremental. Start with the prayer team and begin praying about the weekly services. Remember, style is a tactic, and perhaps one you can vary due to lack of warm bodies or other constraints. Fine. Pray! Remember the Divine Intersection is a means for mission accomplishment. The target is God. I know there are songs, dramas, videos, and other fancy ways to bring this about. But you can do this with well-spoken words, as many fine preachers attest to in their experience.

From the parking lot to the front door, to the ushers, greeters, and people in the worship area, from the music to the multimedia to the drama to the readers to the message to the people praying for the service, from the first touch to the last touch, whether emotional or physical or spiritual, are your people cultivating a capacity for a Divine Intersection in any and all of the ways God might bring that about?

CHAPTER FOUR

TACTICAL STEPS FOR THE DIVINE INTERSECTION

Well, it's Sunday morning and you are getting ready for church. The worship service begins at 10:45 with announcements cleverly projected on the screen, which now covers the organ pipes in the left-hand corner of the church. The announcements are not very important, nothing earth-shattering (youth tonight in the parlor, spaghetti supper in the fellowship hall on Wednesday, and so on). No one pays much attention. After the announcements there is a greeting, a reading of scripture about how great God is, and then the music. By the twenty-minute mark, many are beginning to get in touch, beginning to sense the presence of God. And then we take the offering. The noisy talking resumes, the babies, once quiet, now cry louder, followed by the stares of those who want visitors but not all that noise. By the end of the service, we are so excited we "go home and have lunch."[1]

Or maybe you have a contemporary service. You enter the worship area, the band is playing, people are talking, there are doughnuts in the lobby, and kids are running around. Soon the band gets louder. They do three fast songs, followed by a short time of greeting. Then the band does two slower songs. The drama team enters with a short skit. Then there is the offering, greeting, announcements, then another song, and then the talking head or, if you are really tech savvy, that great PowerPoint presentation. The central theme is presented in many forms: drama, video. There is a closing prayer, the band comes back with the closer, and we all go home and have lunch.

Or maybe you attend a Pentecostal or Charismatic church. The band/music starts and 45 minutes later, all the children have run themselves silly, all the banners are back in place, and we are doing another rendition of that chorus. Then even though you don't have an order of worship or a bulletin, we all can now set our watches because Mary will speak in tongues at exactly 45.3 minutes after the hour followed by Bob giving the same general interpretation: "Thus saith the Lord. My children. I love you with an undying love. Some of you pride yourself for being on the Way. Most of you are simply in the way. Repent. Love Me." The pastor preaches, the choir sings, and we have such a great time. We all leave and go to the restaurant to have lunch.

Certainly Jesus did not go to the cross or rise from the dead so we could beat the Baptists (fill in the church that works for you) to the restaurant. So how can we make our worship experience more meaningful, more transformational, more aware of God's presence, or simply more? I have a few suggestions you might find helpful.

TACTICAL STEPS FOR TRANSFORMATIONAL WORSHIP

Make It a Habit

If you are going to learn to worship in a way that will embrace a Divine Intersection, you will need to make time for God each day. That's right, each day. You can't cultivate a passion for God by ignoring God all week or only giving God a bit of your time each day. It takes time to cultivate this passion for the Divine

Intersection. While it is not a matter of works, it is a matter of cultivation, openness, and the development of a capacity for God.

You will never get great at anything by only doing it occasionally. While many have been saying this about our personal journey with God, I would emphasize this is especially true about our worship of God. If you only worship once a week for twenty minutes, don't expect it to be very meaningful. When I am home and begin my time of worship, it can sometimes take up to twenty minutes for me to get ready to worship. Sometimes I have to sing and play for twenty minutes before I can pray, before I begin to sense that God is near. It isn't that God is not near. God is right there, everywhere. But I have become so numb to God's presence, and so many things (books, TV, Internet, daydreaming) seem to drive me from my relationship with God. It simply takes time, and you must make the time and create the space in your life for worship. Part of the reason this is true for me is that I am so caught up in the world I live in—a world of deadlines, demands, challenges, and unplanned events. In this ever changing world, I get unconnected from the invading God! I get easily lost, disoriented, confused, and, if not careful, I can lose sight of the goal and find myself wandering in the wilderness of my own design. And so on Sunday morning, after a week of a starvation diet with God, I may yearn for that connection but be unable to experience it due to the depleted nature of my soul. I have not developed a space or capacity for a Divine Intersection.

Can you make time each week? Perhaps you are busy and you only have time for a ten-minute connection each day. Great. That is better than nothing for most people. However, it simply doesn't work for me. I need time, twenty minutes to prepare, to make room to be refreshed by God. I need to set aside time and a place where I can be me, where I can come before God in honesty, with no games, and seek God. I need to have a place where I can sing, shout, cry, and express myself. I need time to do that. I can't rush it. And I need to do it more than once a week. I don't do this every day, some days I don't make the time. And my day suffers for it. No, my life suffers for it. However, imposing a new "law" on my life only makes me bitter. I want to spend time with God because of my desire to know and experience God, not to appease a guilt but to express my love and passion for God. And as I make the time, God demonstrates his great love for me by preparing times—Divine Intersections—which transform my life.

Perhaps you aren't musical. Perhaps you don't like listening to worship music. Perhaps you adore the great hymns, classical music, great arias, and recitatives. Perhaps you have other ways to quiet yourself. Some walk or run. Some drop to their knees in their room and practice centering techniques. Some have tried meditation. I would be the last person to say that any one method is right. What works for you? Terry Teykl taught me about prayer temperaments a few years ago.[2] What a great help it was for me to learn I don't have to look like anyone else in my prayers. Some are great on their knees—it puts me to sleep. Some pray for hours focused and intense—I tend to ramble. Some have clear times each day—I vary from day to day. Some use written prayers or poems—I prefer to just talk to God and believe what I say is OK. Some use very polite words—I just talk. What is your prayer temperament? Do you know?

Whatever your style or temperament, what matters is your connection with God. There is no substitute for regular, consistent time spent creating an environment where God can intersect with your life and make a transformative difference.

Dream Bigger Dreams

Carl Sandburg wrote, "Nothing happens unless first a dream!"[3] You may be thinking that the kinds of experiences I am talking about have not been and most likely won't be regular aspects of your worship. I know for sure you won't experience these Divine Intersections if you don't dream about it. What drives you each week as you (and your team) prepare for worship? You have only sixty minutes (ninety minutes on the outside) to create an environment rich in God's presence. You only have this one chance this week to make a transformational impact on someone's life. What keeps you from cultivating this capacity and developing it in your community? "All men dream: but not equally. Those who dream by night in the dusty recesses of their minds wake in the day to find that it was vanity: but the dreamers of the day are dangerous men, for they may act their dream with open eyes, to make it possible."[4]

Focus on the Opportunities

By paying attention to the four dimensions (self, lived world, void, and holy), you will begin to see many opportunities for developing the capacity in others to receive a transforming encounter with God in a Divine Intersection. There are numerous opportunities given to you each day. To be serious pursuers of this transformational process you will have to abandon the notion that you are in control. By paying attention to the four dimensions, particularly the lived world, you and your team will be better able to adjust the "map" of your worship themes as you rub shoulders with real people living real lives in this particular moment in time.

For example, the Sunday following the terrorists' attacks in New York City and Washington D.C., attendance at Sunday services was at an all-time high. People were frightened, confused, angry, and wondering about life in the face of horror like most had never seen. After two weeks, the attendance surge dropped off. Why? Most places on that Sunday could not adjust their "plan" for the circumstance. One church scheduled that Sunday to do their stewardship campaign and no terrorist was going to interfere with that all-important process. Most churches gave people what they usually dish out week after week: eighteenth-century irrelevancies so detached from God that they are sterile, weak, anemic, more of a hospice than a thriving living organism.

At a recent youth festival, I spoke with a twenty-something worship leader. He made these comments to me: "My generation is not interested in pretending. We want to see people who really know God really living for God. We know the answers. We tried church. We find it irrelevant to our needs. My generation is moving from the huge faceless gatherings to the intimacy of the small group that meets in homes. And if the church doesn't soon see the pain we are in and offer worship that addresses our whole existence, we will simply stop coming."

There are numerous opportunities for our congregations to reach out to the people who have never experienced God's reality.

Psychologists tell us that every thirty days a family faces a crisis. Opportunity.

Lives change. Opportunity.

Marriages crumble. Opportunity.

Children are born. Opportunity.

People get older and die. Opportunity.

People lose their jobs and move. Opportunity.

People meet new people, find new passions. Opportunity.

People deal with tragic loss. Opportunity.

People fall in and out of love. Opportunity.

Use each experience as an inroad to preparing people for the encounter that will change their lives.

Use Stories

Use stories about real people to help people identify with life. I know you were told to never talk about yourself from the pulpit. Well first, get out of the pulpit, put away the notes, stop reading to people, and start talking with them. Tell them the true-life stories you have experienced or those you have heard from people you trust. There is something about a true-life story that will prepare you for a Divine Intersection. I was with a pastor who was facing great stress in his congregation. I asked him why he was in ministry, and he told me this story.

"In 1987 I visited Nicaragua for two weeks while the war was going on between the Sandinistas and the Contras. For one week

I stayed in a village that had no 'modern' conveniences and was at the end of the road literally, in the rain forest, or campo. The second day there the body was found of the young village school teacher. He was killed in the cross fire between units of the two groups. It looked like he had been intentionally forced out into the middle of the shooting. I and my traveling companion, a U.S. Catholic priest, said 'words' over his grave (a hole dug where his body was found, his mother laying the best she had—a cheap table cloth—over his body, his young wife and three children with her looking on). No one else in the village wanted to get close, they all stood at least fifty yards away for fear of being considered part of one group or the other and winding up like the teacher.

"I stayed with the Roman Catholic Lay Delegate of the Word and his family in a shack that housed ten of them. He basically served the congregation because a priest only came every six months. He was illiterate. He and his nephew worked a small acreage of corn, five miles away at the base of the mountain. They were cautious because of the fire fights. However, he was more worried about one of his grandchildren inadvertently being in the wrong place at the wrong time.

"In the time I spent with him, I met the living Christ for the first time. He didn't wear Jesus on his sleeve or push him on me so I could be 'saved.' He simply talked about how Jesus Christ was with him in every step with all the danger around. I struggled in my short time there just to survive in the 'primitive' setting. These people faced that and the war with a basic, authentic trust in God. For all my training in college and seminary, all my reading and discussions over thirteen years of ordained ministry to that time, I did not know the Christ that my host and his community knew!

"One night he asked the two of us clergy to visit a smaller shack across the path from his. Even though it was directly across, I hadn't remembered seeing anyone around it. There was a widow, age twenty-one, who lived there with her two young children. Her husband had been killed in the war three months before. But since no 'priest' had been to the town since then, he felt we as 'official' clergy could make a pastoral visit. This home didn't even have the kerosene lantern that our host had. As we talked and the sun set, the room kept getting darker. I don't remember the words; all I remember is that as the night came upon us I knew Christ was present with us. He was real. I had never known that before! Jesus had been an idea I would take off some shelf every Sunday and put in my sermons and then put back on the shelf.

"Thus, beyond all the intellectual knowledge, the mentoring of a man who had never read scripture, and was only hearing it preached every six months by a priest who could read, led me to the living Christ!"[5]

The American pastor, with tears running down his face, told me of the effect of this man on his life and how he had a Divine Intersection, a transforming encounter that night while praying with the lay pastor. This humble lay pastor, who while never having attended one class, let alone a school, had a relationship with God in Christ that sustained and sustains him through life.

I asked him, "Have you ever told that story to your congregation?" He had not. In preaching classes he was instructed to "never talk about himself." I encouraged him to allow others to see why he was so passionate about ministry. Things haven't been the same since.

Aim for the Heart and the Head

So many Sunday morning services are exercises of mental or spiritual gymnastics. What is the point of: standing and sitting, up-down-up-down; back of the book, front of the book, middle of the book, front of the book; words we don't understand or even use anymore; formulas we don't understand; and long intellectually boring monologues?

Most people are bright. They think about everything in their lives. Most people are terribly lonely, searching, wondering, attempting to make sense out of this thing we call life. All the great books, all the attempts at insight have not worked. They have faced the lived world and the void. They have come back searching for assurance, meaning. They want to know if there is really anything worth living for, let alone dying for. And in most congregations the subtle but clear message is something like this: God, who is love, really doesn't like you much, and Jesus, who is the best teacher we ever saw, really isn't saying much that you and I need to know. The point of all this is that we might be better people and so "hope to die on a day when God is in a good mood."[6] But, until that time could you please come and give at least your money? Well, you don't need to come much. And could you keep those noisy children at home?

Or could you imagine a place where people have been praying all week that you might have a Divine Intersection, a radically transforming experience with God in various forms, in many types of styles and interactions? In one corner of the room you might find joyful singing, in another corner deep prayer, and in another corner you might find a "life drama." In the rear of the room you might find food with tables and places for conversation around holographic images projected in the center of the table. Perhaps these images would be of a mission team "live" in some part of the world. In another part of the room you might find a group involved in a study of relevant life issues. Can you imagine a place where all four dimensions of life are embraced, where even the negatives can be negated through the transforming power of Jesus?

Speak Indigenously

Good friends of mine felt a calling to go to Kenya to work with a mission group in that country. So, years before they were to leave they began to prepare. Their preparation included learning to speak Swahili and Massai. Imagine going to a country so different in culture, language, and meaning and making the fatal mistake that the people there would learn to understand you. Most of us know the mission field is right at our door. When we step from our homes we enter the mission field. So they learned to speak and listen to new languages. It was crucial for them to speak indigenously, in the language of the people they were living with. It was crucial that when they spoke, people could understand them.

In the United States (and most of western Europe), most don't know what we believe or why. Those long intellectual treatises aren't doing much to help many. On many Sundays and especially at those congregations that believe the sermon is the "keystone" to the service, I often find myself taking a time trip back two hundred years or more. The language is cumbersome. Many terms will be defined: words like *eschatology, soteriology, ultimate concern, real presence, consubstantiated,* and so on. Sure, in seminary, graduate students learn the minutia about these terms, and many discussions there would be impossible without the years spent defining and redefining the terminology. The same is true of many disciplines: medicine, psychology, physiology, on and on. When the doctor emerges from the emergency room, I don't need a lecture on the various valves and complications of valves in the heart. I don't need to know all the technical terms they use in that room. I need to hear the doctor tell me, in terms I can understand, what happened, what is going on, and what might happen (diagnosis, treatment plan, and prognosis). I *might* know "myocardial infarction." I *do* know "heart attack." Aren't lawyers the only people we pay to confuse us? ;-) It shouldn't be the church.

Let me be practical. If you have to define terms in your morning service, odds are you are speaking the wrong language. People come looking for hope, not terms they don't understand.[7] If you read long passages from books of great thinkers, odds are you have lost the congregation by the second sentence. It takes tremendous practice to read in a way that is inviting and intriguing.[8]

If you stand behind a pulpit and read your notes, most visitors will not return. If you are going to keep the Sunday morning monologues, try memorizing your message. Try this schedule: Monday, look at the theme the team is working on and what is the pivotal point that you will address in the message. Outline the passages you will use. Tuesday, write the message out in full.

Wednesday, revise and begin to memorize the key points. Thursday, polish the message. Stand in front of a mirror or video-tape yourself delivering this message.[9] Long passages from other sources can be on cards, but the fewer you use the better off you are. Friday, allow for a day off. Saturday night, pick the manu-script back up, edit, and polish it, making sure you have all the key points down. Sunday, take the manuscript with you but don't look at it unless you are lost. Instead, look into the eyes of the people you are talking to. How many of them make eye contact with you? How close are you to speaking to them about their self, lived world, and void? How are you preparing them for a Divine Intersection by speaking their language and doing it in a way that is honest, powerful, and right from your heart?

Is this scary? Sure. Going in front of people week after week and talking to them is a scary thing. If you have been used to using a wheelchair, standing without a cane is hard. In a matter of a few months you will have this process down. And while you are at it, why not mentor three or four other people to do this so you don't have to be the only one? I know that is more scary than going without notes. We need to use all the intellectual acumen we can and use it to learn how to share the wonderful news of God's love in a language many of us don't speak (and sadly a lot don't want to learn). I'm not suggesting you try to speak like the group you are trying to reach. I frankly can't do hip-hop. But can I learn to listen to their heart cries and then help my team to develop environments where a Divine Intersection might hap-pen to this group?

A large church in the Midwest was struggling. This very tradi-tional church had recently moved to a new site directly off the new interstate loop. Easy access and a new building were key fac-tors in the decision to relocate to this place. Yet this congrega-tion was not attracting many of the huge numbers of people who were buying land, building houses, and moving to this area. As I spent three days with them it was clear they had major issues. First, they used to be a family church in a small village. Now they were a large church on the edge of urban growth. Second, they had no clue who they were or how to organize. They were unclear of purpose, principles, and people[10] and they were organized to decline, using patterns for organization that came out of the 1700s and were designed for congregations that worship fewer than one hundred.[11] Third, their worship was not user-friendly nor was it very transformational. After gaining clarity about their purpose and principles, these people organized in a new stream-lined manner, and out of that organizational structure many changes were made in worship. The combination of these ordinary people with a clear purpose and clear principles together with an empowering system for mobilizing each person to thrive in ministry allowed the pastor and worship team to design and implement worship experiences that were aimed at head and heart. The result was spiritual growth by those already there, great passion for their purpose, a new way to "do" ministry and a new outlook on worship. What a difference that has made. Now they are faced with great problems: they need more land. They need staff. They need the denomination to not interfere by "fix-ing" something that is not broken.[12]

A small Lutheran congregation, very traditional and very much in decline, called a new pastor with a new vision to lead them. This pastor was clear about purpose and principle and came to them with ideas about reaching all those people "that no one else wants." They began to pray. They began to dream. They began a new worship experience that looked like the community they were attempting to be in ministry with. They brought gui-tars, drums, bass, and other instruments. They moved the pulpit out. They rearranged the seating, moving from pews to comfort-able chairs. They still offered the traditional Lutheran service at 8:00 on Sunday mornings. They also offered a more contempo-rary worship experience at 10:30. Many of the traditionalists got fed up and left. Changing worship just to reach people did not appeal to them. Church is about us, our needs, our wants, and if we don't get it we will leave. The church was struggling before, but with the loss of many people the church hit harder times. The pastor took cuts in pay, convinced that the new service would reach many more people. Fabulous things happened in this place. The worship team was outstanding. They were speaking the language of the community. Many people came to the later service. But that made some in the early service angry. More left. The early service took on a blended feel: still very Lutheran but now with newer music and PowerPoint graphics. The later service had new people, new gifts, and talents hungering to be used. It has been hard work, but recently that pastor wrote me. He said he is amazed at how God is working in this congregation. Many of those people were hardened by life. Many were on the edge of life, not sure life was worth it. Now, they are going to the home-less, working with those addicted, caring for their neighbors, reaching out to those at work. Many of these people have been through divorce, addiction, hurt, and pain that rips your heart. Because this worship team has made intentional room for God, lives are being changed. The change has been hard. Many dear friends have parted ways. If you aren't serious about your purpose you won't get through the hard times. If you aren't regularly experiencing Divine Intersections and life transformation, why would you want to?

In a house in Indianapolis, twelve people gather to pray, share, worship, and care for each other. They are young, middle-aged, and older. They are single, married, and divorced. They are growing in their love for God and each other. They spend most of their time in worship and prayer. They have learned to be open to the Divine Intersection. They have experienced many such Intersections while singing, praying, or just being quiet with each other. They are facing a difficult decision, a choice to grow and expand their group. They have gotten very close to each other. They are not unique. There are thirty such groups who have joined together for common purpose, sharing common principles. Growth is usually painful. They have learned to pray and to hold each other through the changes that life brings. They have learned to worship, making room for God to encounter them in their daily lives as well as in the small group or corporate worship on Sunday. One clear learning experience sticks out to me here: they have learned how to make room for a Divine Intersection in the small groups that meet midweek. In these encounters they have learned to listen and to hear God and to act on what they hear. Someone needs prayer, they pray. Someone needs to cry out their pain, they hold them, care for them, and allow them to have their time with God. They have become more aware and more ready for a Divine Intersection in their lives. This naturally flows over to their larger gathering on Sunday. They can take others publicly because they have been there privately. The language they use is common, you won't need a dictionary when you are with them. They are bright, articulate, educated, and passionate about reaching the world for Jesus Christ using small, home-based cell groups as the vehicle to reach people.[13]

Understand That Music Is the Ritual

While not limited to music, the main avenue for preparing people for a Divine Intersection will be through music and visuals. The combination seems to work particularly well with people in the United States in that for the last fifty years each generation has grown up with both movies and television, and now we are adding computer Web pages, in which visual and auditory expressions are used to convey both important and trivial items. Given the many different ways people learn, you would be wise to consider how visual learners might be helped in your worship by providing projected images that correlate with the morning's theme.

Again, the style of the music is only a tool. Any style can be a vehicle for God to invade our reality. The crucial aspect is not the style of music but the message it conveys. Some hymns as well as some contemporary songs are not a good fit and hinder the ability to develop a capacity for a Divine Intersection. I remember one community Good Friday service where a local church brought a soloist to sing following one of the scripture readings in the service. The Christmas carol she sang destroyed the service for me. "Come On, Ring Those Bells" just did not fit with the solemnity of the Good Friday service. However at another Good Friday service the contemporary chorus "Nails in Your Hands" was made even more meaningful by the distribution of small cut nails which were the "reverse offering" for that service. That is, plates were passed out to give nails to each person. Instead of taking a monetary offering, people were asked to take the nails from the plate as their offering, symbolic of the self-sacrifice each would be giving in response to the sacrifice Jesus made on our behalf on the cross. The song made real the sacrifice of Jesus both in words and by the visual images on the screen. The experience was enhanced by the symbolic device (nails) that people could take with them from the service. The closing song in that service was the old spiritual "Were You There," made even more powerful by the dimming of lights and the stripping[14] of all objects from the worship center except the small spotlight on a wooden cross with a crown of thorns and a nail.

Music seems to be a constant presence in most lives. Music needs to undergird the entire worship experience. Most worship experiences will be helped by the underlying use of music throughout the service. Most people start and end every day with music playing. Radio alarms wake us and the radio puts us to sleep. During the day, we play music from many sources. At home, on the road, in the doctor's office, in the elevator, in the store, and in the workplace, music is constant. Raised in this environment, I have music as my constant companion as well. In the car, on the plane, in the airport, on the way to worship, before worship, and after worship, I will have music playing. When there isn't music the silence is deadening. My children are likewise wired for sound, carrying their CD players and now MP3 players wherever they go. You will not find many people today who are not surrounded by music, all kinds of music. Music is the ritual and liturgy of their lives.

Worship used to be much more musically attuned. Methodists were noted for their loud, joyful singing. The camp meeting was a place were hymn sings were regularly the first hour of the evening service. Many congregations used to host regular organ recitals that were primarily worship music. One of my friends continues to draw large crowds for his organ recitals. The music is mostly written by people who have a faith and who worship regularly. He plays weekly for worship. It is a part of his life.[15]

Music, no matter the style, is the ritual. Music is the primary means by which we are invited into that place where Divine Intersections occur. Music is the primary means by which our lives are touched. Someone once told me that the human voice in song is the best proof of God's existence.

As a freshman in college with some interest in music, I auditioned for the college touring choir. I was surprised I made it, and even more surprised to learn that this Methodist-related college had the only choir in the region that regularly sang the Latin Mass for Roman Catholic congregations. Learning and singing the *Missa brevis* in D minor by Mozart was a terrific learning experience. Once while leading a congregation in worship, we were singing the *Agnus Dei* portion of the mass when the presence of God seemed so thick you could cut it with a knife. Many in the choir were visibly touched, as were many of the people in the congregation. Reading the words as we sang the section (few know Latin any more, even among the Roman Catholic Church), those in the worship center were touched by the combination of Mozart's score, the visual appeal of the interior of this Catholic church, and the sound of human voices singing their best to God's glory. These elements converged to produce an atmosphere ripe for a Divine Intersection. Unfortunately, the Priest did not have a clue what to do with this experience. It wasn't in the bulletin and wasn't a scheduled part of the Divine Liturgy. Why is it that worship, which was originally a place where the glory of God was present and expected, is now a place where God's presence is rarely experienced and seldom expected? What a terrible turn of events.

Each week Robert Schuller produces a worship experience with an eye toward God's direct intervention in the lives of the people gathered or watching that morning. The *Hour of Power* has mastered the use of music and visuals. Hymns, special music, new choruses, orchestrations, brass, and electric instruments augment the fabulous sounds of the sanctuary organ. The music is excellently done, and you know these people aren't "just performing," they are worshiping. There may be much you don't like about television worship, and there are many on television that frankly turn me off, but the *Hour of Power* is not one of those for me. Watch this worship soon. Get past what you don't like and experience the way music and visuals are used to bring people to a place where they might encounter God in a transformational way.

There are worship DVDs available now, most notably iWorship from Integrity Music.[16] These enhanced CDs are designed to facilitate worship toward a Divine Intersection. The combination of great songs and eye-catching visuals (at a very affordable price) is making the use of this type of media possible for even small congregations. Worship Leader is also marketing a "worship resource kit" featuring Matt and Sherry McPherson. This project has a DVD music video, an enhanced CD, sound tracks, lead sheets, a music chart, and a PowerPoint presentation.

Worship videos like *Passion: OneDay Live* are available at most Christian bookstores and through the Internet. These DVDs feature music and teaching with powerful spontaneous worship services. The teaching segments can be long but worth the watching as you will find numerous speakers creating an atmosphere and capacity for their worshipers to experience a Divine Intersection. The double-sided DVDs also have featured songs with surround mixes that enhance the songs and the experience. I have watched some of these segments dozens of times and each time been drawn into the presence of God.

Worship Leader Magazine is a terrific resource as well.[17] There are great articles, reviews of new books and worship songs, worship tech solutions, and contributions from Robert Webber and Sally Morgenthaler. Worship Leader also has a bi-monthly service called *Song DISCovery*.[18] Each bi-monthly worship service resource offers a CD with new songs from known and newly discovered artists. There are worship settings, prepared PowerPoint slides of all the songs, lead sheets in PDF format, and a magazine with lead sheets and very practical articles to improve your worship.

Hosanna! Music also offers a monthly subscription to a worship resource.[19] Top names like Paul Baloche, Don Moen, Ron Kenoly, Lenny LeBlanc, Tommy Walker, and Jami Smith (and many more) are represented. Each month you receive a CD with instrumental instruction, videos, and chord charts with lyrics. You also will get a songbook with overhead masters and music charts for piano and guitar.

Vision Magazine is devoted to "ministering through multimedia."[20] While a relative newcomer to the worship magazine field, it has great articles and many helpful advertisements of products to enhance your worship. This magazine is loaded with multimedia Web sites and advertising guaranteed to help you make the most of your money and your time.

Of course the use of any of this material is dependent on your current subscription to their service and a current subscription to Christian Copyright License International.[21] To use the video material you will also need a motion picture license. Please check with the agency regarding the legality of your use of the material. You may have to write directly to the owner of the copyright and request permission to use a given resource. There may be fees to pay and guidelines to follow. Each media element you are using has its own special set of rules.

I cannot close without reminding you of the other side of the spectrum: silence. Silence must not be overlooked. Silence will be more powerful when sparingly and purposefully used. There is a time for all things, a place for all things. As we intentionally move toward developing a capacity to experience a Divine Intersection in our lives your use of silence will be crucial. I would err on the side of little silence until you are more aware of God's intersection in your worship. There was a time a few months ago when we were singing about God's holiness. As the chorus repeated, "You are holy, you are holy," the singing became softer, gradually decreasing in volume. When it was not much more than a whisper, it was clear we were in a time when we needed to be "still and know." The next few moments of silence were wonderfully refreshing.

CHAPTER FIVE

POSSIBLE PITFALLS

Possible pitfalls in an attempt to recognize the central importance of God being an active player (and not a passive observer) in our worship would be anything that would cause deviation from the purpose and principles of the gathered assembly. If the congregation has discerned that their purpose is "to bring people into a relationship with God in Christ and repeat this process in others," then the organization and use of the people of the congregation to promote and hold a concert or a recital to "raise money for the operational budget" is a violation of the purpose. Remember, raising money is never the purpose, never even a side road to the purpose. As I have said earlier, the foundational level for all community gatherings is based on the leadership's and the community's *understanding of and commitment to* the purpose, the congregation's reason for existence. The principles, which include the values and beliefs, motivate this congregation to accomplish its purpose or mission. Nothing matters if the purpose of the community is not accomplished. It is *all about the purpose!* Everything the congregation attempts must fulfill its purpose. There is no justification for anything that does not accomplish this purpose. Having a craft fair to raise money to pay the heating bills is not the purpose of the congregation. Anything that fails to accomplish the purpose is a waste of something much more valuable than money: our time.

PITFALL 1: SURVIVAL MENTALITY

Once a community loses sight of its purpose, it is a short step to irrelevancy. So many communities older than five years have strayed from their purpose and face certain decline. How many of our great colleges and institutions (like the YMCA) once had a very clear disciple-making purpose but now are civic organizations with almost nothing that resembles the passion on which they were founded? One well-established congregation became known as the "turkey supper church." What an honor! When I asked about the now historic turkey suppers, I was told these dinners were held to raise money. For what? To buy turkeys! It was the sum and substance of their passion. In another congregation it was the "Women's Society Bazaar" held every year to "raise money to support the church." Yet no one was ever allowed to see their treasurer's books. After a huge fight the pastor was told, "That money belongs to us, not to the church, and we can use it any way we want."

At one congregation they insisted they could not pay their pastor. They had to raise money through bake sales, bazaars, fundraisers, and suppers. For three months the pastor was not paid. The pastor then slipped a one hundred dollar bill in the offering plate. The next week at the council meeting there was no record of the donation in the weekly accounting. Curious, the pastor called the bank and asked what the balance was in the accounts. After clearing with the bank management that this person was the pastor, he was asked, "Which account? You have three under that name." The pastor asked to hear what the balance was in each one. Shocked to learn that this rural congregation had over $35,000 in the bank, it became clear that at least the treasurer of this congregation knew principles were being violated. This church had become so worried about survival they were willing to lie about their financial health rather than focus on the mission.

Once the foundational elements are neglected, the church begins to morph into a club, and in that arena there would be little passion for the mission. It becomes about survival! In environments where there is no passion for the mission, why would transformational encounters with God be anything but suspicious and terrorizing? After all, God might call us to leave the comfort we have and travel to some unknown place like south Philadelphia, Harlem, or Los Angeles. I have found that most missionless and passionless communities would rather die than have God invade their comfort and ease. All that matters to them is that they survive.

PITFALL 2: BECOMING ADDICTS TO AN EXPERIENCE

Another possible pitfall in attempting to develop a capacity and receptivity for regular experiences of the Divine Intersection is that we will make the experience the target. I believe this is one of the chief difficulties facing many congregations who tend to be open to the more "emotional" aspects of worship. Often these congregations will have an emotional experience and build their entire worship and structure on repeating that experience. Erring on this side has its consequences. Emotionalism detached from principles (values and beliefs) will lead to disaster. If you make the emotional aspects of God's Divine Intersection the goal, you will eventually be no different from drug addicts who go from high to high without ever accomplishing anything. Congregations who focus on the experience create an idolatrous system in which they worship the experience instead of God. The purpose of creating a capacity for a Divine Intersection is always for transformation of our lives into greater effectiveness for fulfillment of the purpose within the principles of the congregation.

PITFALL 3: NEGLECTING THE PURPOSE OR PRINCIPLES IN PURSUIT OF THE EXPERIENCE

If the purpose is to make disciples, then everything we do must be evaluated in light of this mission. Sure, worship may cause us to forget some social conveniences. King David danced naked before the Lord. While David's wife was embarrassed, God in fact seemed pleased. George Fox[1] placed his feet in the fire, was not burned, but soon burned up the land with his experiences of God.[2] Many have left homes, loved ones, fame, fortune, and ease for the sake of the gospel. I have been continually inspired by people like Jim and Elisabeth Elliot, Nate Saint, Corrie ten Boom, and more modern examples like Clare Good, Mike Skelton, Vicki Kelly, Bruce Cole, Pam Princell, and Gilbert Kingsley.[3] A pivotal question to ask yourself and others is, "with your first breath or your last penny, will it be you or the mission?"[4]

The purpose is the administrative rule of the individual and the community. If we fail to keep the purpose, we will fail to be effective and all the efforts at transformational worship will end in disappointment. If you lose sight of the purpose or replace the purpose with any other "goal" you will find that the Spirit will move on. I have not found that God is easily manipulated by our fear, lack of faith, or insecurities. I have seen great worship ruined by the continual faithless plea for money. If God is calling you to expand your outreach or your facilities, it has been my experience that these things should not interfere with the ongoing ministry of the congregation. If it does it is usually because of the faithlessness of the leadership or, more commonly, the mistaken belief that you can abandon purpose for a season to raise money. It never works. Growth usually stops, finances become tighter, and key people leave, unable to bear the lack of congruence between the stated principles and the lived principles.

A congregation cannot go against or violate its principles without experiencing harm. Like cogs in a gear, each time we violate a principle we will throw debris into the way the entire process works, gradually destroying the way the organism functions. You can't build teams with top-down command and power-hungry people. You can't make room for God or develop a capacity for a Divine Intersection in a worship service in which leaders manipulate people. Likewise you can't develop a capacity for a Divine Intersection when the leaders control people and have trouble with emotion or with spontaneity. If you can't live your principles, your worship will reflect that lack of trust and lack of integrity as your "ideal" does not match the "real."

PITFALL 4: APATHY ABOUT TRANSFORMATION

Another pitfall, and perhaps the most common, is the general apathy in most congregations toward anything that even speaks of the transformation of lives in Jesus Christ. I was with a group of pastors in the Northeast and was sharing some of my concerns about their apathy and disconnectedness from any life-changing purpose to make disciples for Jesus Christ. The pastors that had gathered represented twenty-five congregations. In the last three years, two people found new life in Christ out of twenty of the congregations combined. We spent the morning talking about purpose and principles, which lead to more effective ways of helping people connect with Jesus Christ. One of their judicatory leaders got me aside later that day and asked if I could please stop talking about Jesus so much. Actually he said, "If you don't stop talking about Jesus I will puke." While many faithful pew sitters won't have the boldness to say things like this, they think them. What is all this fuss about purpose, Jesus, discipleship? Why can't we just have worship the way it was in 1959 or 1974? Why can't the pastor read from *I'm Okay, You're Okay* and just leave all the "Jesus stuff" out? Why can't we just gather, sing a few great songs (like "How Great Thou Art"—no, too conservative; how about "God of Love and God of Power"—no, too activist; how about "O for a Thousand Tongues"—no, could be construed to sympathize with pentecostalism; OK, so we won't sing) and call it a day? Do you really have to talk about Jesus so much?

It is my conviction, and one shared by many of my mentors and peers, that as in the first century, the central issue is Christology. To that end I am so helped by James Charlesworth.[5] He writes, "We continue to proclaim what the earliest Jews who followed Jesus claimed: a story about Jesus the Christ that is not interesting fiction but inviting history."[6] Clearly the topic is central to the unbelieving world. The popularity of Mel Gibson's *Passion of the Christ* is due in part to the general ignorance of who Jesus was and is and his place in the formation of this new expression of God's grace called Christianity. So to answer the question of the judicatory person, to stop talking about Jesus is to stop talking, for there is no other name, no other person, no Other that has the words, the life-giving words. For me it is all about Jesus. Christology is the issue. The Divine Intersection is the invasion of God, who, in Jesus, has invaded our reality and who, through the Holy Spirit, comes into our three dimensions of existence (self, lived world, and void) in such a way that anyone so affected by this invasion will be forever changed and transformed. "Now we look inside, and what we see is that anyone united with the Messiah gets a fresh start, is created new. The old life is gone; a new life burgeons!" (2 Cor 5:17 *Message*). I can't talk about transformation, let alone Divine Intersection, without talking about Jesus.

"Work hard for sin your whole life and your pension is death" (Rom 6:23 *Message*). While wonderfully ecstatic experiences have been part of the landscape of American expressions of Christianity (Shakers), eventually the values were crossed, beliefs were modified for the sake of progress, and the purpose soon disappeared. Anything that causes a worshiping community to deviate from the purpose (and for me that is making disciples of Jesus Christ) would create an entity in which Divine Intersections would not and could not occur. Why would God bless that which doesn't accomplish the purpose God gave the best for? Why would God send these wonderful life-changing experiences into a community who cared little for God's purposes in this world? Of what benefit are transformational experiences if not for the furthering of transformation in the world?

EPILOGUE

I am sitting at my kitchen table watching the sun rise on a beautiful Sunday morning winter scene. Christmas is long past, the "bleak midwinter" is upon us, water stands "like a stone."[1]

What has been most revealing to me is how I dread Sundays when I'll go to worship and hear one more irrelevant message with a group of people who aren't welcoming, who seem to enjoy rules and regulations more than they enjoy Jesus. It seems like this at almost every congregation I visit. I recognize that I don't get to see many healthy congregations. That is my job: going to the hurting and declining congregations and bringing a new way, a new hope, a new experience.

I am home this weekend and so we will attend the new congregation we are a part of. They have great hearts, a great purpose, and a passion to live their principles. They have brought much "church" with them. Some call it baggage. I call it sewage. Like Paul said, "I consider them rubbish"—sewage if you will (Phil 3:8 NIV). They are learning to leave much of it behind as they focus on their purpose and principles and as they develop a capacity for Divine Intersections. They are willing to learn. I have been teaching (and learning with) their leaders how to be sensitive to God's leading, how to focus on each aspect: self, lived world, void, and holy. As they pay direct attention to these things, their worship is changing. They are following Jesus better. They are praying. They are worshiping with head and heart. They show potential.

As I sit at home I am typing, listening, and watching the wildlife outside my window. I am listening to a worship CD and here in my home I am caught up, a Divine Intersection is occurring, again. I am aware of me (self), my needs and those of my family, my pain and their pain. I am aware of this world (lived world) in all its beauty and agony. I am aware of the pain (void)—it is heavy upon me. I want rock solid, and all we get is gelatin at best. Yet through the moment there is also this One (holy) who is knocking at my heart, my vile, sinful, and joyful heart. I am aware there is purpose. It is getting clearer as the fog settles. I am aware of principles: prayer, teams, integrity, accountability, small groups, God's love, Jesus is Lord, the Holy Spirit is for today. I am aware of people, gifted people, loving people, waiting for a chance to live for Jesus with all their hearts.

I know for me these Divine Intersections are crucial. I can't live this life without God's direct encounter in my life. And at each area—self, lived world, and even void—I am aware there is One over, above, beyond, inside, outside, under, and through it all who will be there, no matter what!

In writing this book I have felt as if I was saying something so obvious as to be ridiculous. Yet, in my work, I travel to many congregations each year who have demonstrated to me that their worship is so empty of God's presence.

The people in our churches need the life-transforming presence of God in their lives. How could this movement that spread like wildfire be reduced to a few sparks scattered across the land? I believe that as we are willing to risk and pay more attention to the four dimensions necessary for the invasion of God into our worship and lives, we will see the return of the wildfire in our land. God is moving. God desires to be moving in your community, in your gatherings, in ways that might make you uncomfortable, but in ways that will change your lives.

I hope your life is filled with Divine Intersections. If I can help you and your congregation, don't hesitate to call or e-mail me. You can find more information at my Web site www.jhpconsult ing.com.

A BRIEF EXPERIMENT IN
DIVINE INTERSECTION

In order to facilitate your own experience of a Divine Intersection I would ask that you obtain the following songs and listen to them in the order they are listed. Most of the songs can be found on Michael W. Smith's *Worship* CD. The order is not crucial but is my suggestion to help you develop a capacity to experience God's presence in a transformational way. If you don't have access to that CD try these: Jami Smith, *Wash Over Me*; Matt Redman, *Facedown*; or Integrity's *House of Worship*. If none of those CDs are available to you, you can sign on to iTunes music store where I have arranged an iMix collection of these songs for you. You will have to download them at a cost of ninety-nine cents per song.[1]

- "Breathe"
- "Above All"
- "Open the Eyes of My Heart"
- "Seeing You"
- "There Is a Reason"
- "Dancing Generation"

OK, you have the songs. Now, find a place where you can be comfortable. Sit with your feet flat on the floor. Think about your life for a few moments.

Self—What are you personally going through? What issues are pressing in around you? What hurts? What is wonderful? Where do you need God?

Lived World—Think about this world for a few moments. What is wonderful about life today? What is painful? What is simply frustrating? What in this world impinges on you?

Void—Where are you struggling? Where is life more sour than sweet?

Start the songs. "Breathe."

As the song starts, begin taking slow, deep breaths. Allow the sounds of the guitar to help you. Take a deep breath. As the song continues, take numerous deep breaths. Don't sing along. As the song progresses, imagine you are standing before Jesus. Look into his eyes. See his face. Look at him. Can you tell him how desperate you are for him? Can you tell him how lost you are, how much you need him? Where would your life be without Jesus?

Take a deep breath. Breathe deeply again. Breathe again. Enjoy the music.

As the music goes to the next song, relax. Don't stop the music. Breathe. And now listen to the words of "Above All."

Above all things, above the pain of life, above all you have ever known, God has been looking for you. Above all things God has ever done, all the wonders, the wealth, the treasures of the earth, there is no way to measure what God is worth. And in God demonstrating his love for us, no better image comes to mind than Jesus on the cross. Crucified, dead, and buried. He lived to die, rejected and alone. Like a rose trampled on the ground. He took the fall, and thought of you above all. He embraced the void for you, embraced all that would destroy meaning, and thought of you and me.

"There Is a Reason," performed by Alison Krauss and written by Ron Block (who plays guitar for Alison Krauss and Union Station), sums up so much of the void experiences in my life. I put this song on this list for those of you like me who wonder about the pain of life, who know that life ought to be so much more but who each day are reminded that many children die before they reach twelve years of age. After the twin towers collapsed this was the song I sang to help me. What is the reason for the voids in our lives? Why do we do stupid things, hurt those we love, even turning our backs on God and those dear for moments of fleeting delight? Why do we keep seeking life from death, when the One "who loves me most" would give me all? I "do believe, but help my unbelief."

Take a deep breath. Have you felt it yet? I have had numerous moments in listening to these words, these sounds, seeing my life (self), my experience (lived world), the void (both from without and from within) when I have sensed Jesus near (the holy). I have felt the urge to cry, to run to God, and to fling myself at his feet thinking that somehow when I bring my heart to God, God will mend the brokenness, give peace in the storm and protection from the battles. But in all these things I know he calls me to open my eyes to those around me who have nowhere to run in their pain. I know he calls me on toward the fulfillment of the mission, that all might know Jesus, because only in Jesus can there be life in this death and decay. Only in Jesus is the negative negated, and the world, while never made right, is this time and place where we all can know the love of God, "which passes knowledge."

You might want to end here, or you can listen to the rest of the songs. End with "Dancing Generation" or "Seeing You," then try being quiet for a few moments. If you have experienced God drawing near, what are you discerning about your life, your relationships with God and others, and the call God has on your life? What is God saying, conveying to you? How are you being changed by this experience? I would love to hear about your experience. E-mail me at jeff@jhpconsulting.com; let me know.

NOTES

Introduction

1. MercyMe, "I Can Only Imagine," INO Records, 2001.
2. Chris Rice, "Untitled Hymn (Come to Jesus)," Rocketown Records, 2004.

1. The Divine Intersection

1. James Loder, *The Transforming Moment: Understanding Convictional Experiences* (San Francisco: Harper and Row, 1981), 66.
2. Ibid., 1-6.
3. C. S. Lewis, *A Grief Observed* (New York: Seabury Press, 1961), 9.
4. Loder, *Transforming Moment*, 66.
5. Søren Kierkegaard, *Fear and Trembling and The Sickness Unto Death* (trans. Walter Lowrie; Princeton: Princeton University Press, 1941), 146-47.
6. Loder, *Transforming Moment*, 76.
7. Ibid., 79, 83.
8. Ibid., 90.
9. Ibid., 27.
10. Overchurched—people who have been burnt out by congregational life and who, while they have been in worship/congregational life for most of their lives, have not had an encounter they would describe as transformational.
11. Big Daddy Weave, "Fields of Grace," on *Song DISCovery*, vol. 43, Hosanna! Music, 2004.
12. The direction of the song is a crucial aspect in worship. Once you

move your attention from self and lived world to the holy, keep the focus on holy. Don't mix the directions as it will break the flow and concentration of the worshiper and hinder the chance of experiencing a Divine Intersection.

13. Matt Redman, "You Are Worthy," Sparrow Records, 2004.

14. Max Lucado, *No Wonder They Call Him the Savior* (Portland: Multnomah Press, 1986), 159.

2. Preparing for a Divine Intersection

1. Evanescence, "Tourniquet," Wind-up Records, 2003.

2. *Jesus Christ Superstar* by Andrew Lloyd Webber and Tim Rice was a major factor in my journey. Hearing the ancient story told in music I could hear caused me to listen in a new way. In this musical I heard of a God who did not have all the answers but who understood pain, life, meaning, the world and in some way was saying, "I am still here."

3. Terry Teykl is a prayer evangelist and author of numerous books on prayer. His Web site, www.renewalministries.com, has all the information you need on Terry and his services.

4. Delirious is a British worship band. They have a tremendous grasp of worship. Songs such as "Lord You Have My Heart," "Follow," "Deeper," "Shout to the North," "Majesty," and "Inside Outside" are among some of their more popular songs.

5. Passion is an outreach ministry to college-age people. The Web site, www.passionnow.org/enter.shtml or www.268generation.com, features worship leaders like Jami Smith, Chris Tomlin and Matt Redman.

6. *Titanic*, directed by James Cameron (Hollywood: Twentieth Century Fox and Paramount Pictures, 1997). You will need a license to show portions of the film to the public. To obtain a license, contact Motion Picture Licensing Corporation, 5455 Centinela Avenue, Los Angeles, CA 90066-6970, TEL: (800) 462-8855, (310) 822-8855, FAX: (310) 822-4440, e-mail: info@mplc.com, or visit the Web site: www.mplc.com.

7. Audio Adrenaline, "It Is Well with My Soul," Forefront Records, 1999.

8. Debby Boone, "Heart of the Matter," Lamb and Lion Records, 1985.

9. The Shorter Catechism of the Westminster Assembly, Published for the General Assembly by the Program Agency of the United Presbyterian Church in the United States of America.

10. Terry Teykl, *Blueprint for the House of Prayer* (Muncie, Ind.: Prayer Point Press, 1999). Also see www.prayerguide.org.uk/actsmodel.htm.

11. For a detailed study of this phenomenon of Wintergreen LifeSavers, do a search on the Internet.

12. Terry Teykl, *The Presence Based Church* (Muncie, Ind.: Prayer Point Press, 2003).

13. Ibid., 11.

14. Ibid., 12.

3. Designing Worship for Divine Intersection

1. Lee Ann Womack, "I Hope You Dance," MCA, 2000.

2. Particularly Eric Haines of Digital Media Arts, Williamsport, Pennsylvania, ericjhaines1@suscom.net.

3. Chris Tomlin, J. D. Walt, and Jesse Reeves, "The Wonderful Cross," Sixsteps Music, 2000.

4. Philip Yancey, *The Jesus I Never Knew* (Grand Rapids, Mich.: Zondervan, 1995).

5. C. S. Lewis, *The Lion, the Witch and the Wardrobe* (*The Chronicles of Narnia*; New York: Collier Books, 1950), 75.

6. Walt Kallestad, *Entertainment Evangelism: Taking the Church Public* (Nashville: Abingdon Press, 1996). This is a great book about making Christ and church accessible to a pre-Christian and unreached world.

7. I also practice what I call the five essentials of leadership:
I pray as much as I can. I have a regular devotional time; I worship regularly.
I am involved in small groups.
I involve myself in hands-on social justice. I personally go to a men's shelter and rub shoulders with men who are very different from me.
I worship regularly with others.
I practice stewardship of time, talents, and resources. See www.horizons stewardship.com for terrific resources to improve stewardship habits of your congregation.

8. This worship service of fifty minutes will include musical chanting, healing prayers, and the opportunity to practice the presence of God and to listen to God in prayer. This form of worship began in Taizé, France. Brother Roger, a native of Switzerland, felt called by God to help people in trouble during World War II. He bought a house in Taizé to use for welcoming refugees and others in crisis. He was forced to leave

for two years, and, when he returned, others had joined him. Today thousands of people, especially youth and young adults, are drawn from around the world to join in the rhythm of the community's prayer and small group offerings.

9. Dan Kimball, *The Emerging Church* (Grand Rapids, Mich.: Zondervan, 2003) and *Emerging Worship* (Grand Rapids, Mich.: Zondervan, 2004).

10. William M. Easum and Thomas G. Bandy, *Growing Spiritual Redwoods* (Nashville: Abingdon Press, 1997). A plan is inflexible and unable to adapt to societal changes. A map gives a broader perspective to reach a destination from many different directions.

11. Dee Hock, *Birth of the Chaordic Age* (San Francisco: Berrett-Koehler Publishers, 1999). Another author, Thomas Bandy, talks about four elements in the DNA (*Vision Discernment Workbook*, available through www.easumbandy.com). Bandy's terms (core values, bedrock beliefs, motivational vision, and key mission) all work together to help a person or a congregation understand its purpose and call. I understand purpose to be somewhat like key mission. Purpose and mission answer the question, *why are we here?* Principles are both values and faith convictions or beliefs. In a practical expression of these terms I would offer the following: My purpose or key mission is "that all might know Jesus" (Phil 3:10 and Matt 28:20). Among my principles are my values (prayer, honesty, integrity, accountability, hands-on social justice, and teams) and my faith convictions (God's love is unconditional, Jesus is Lord, and the Holy Spirit is active and moving in our lives and in the church today). The motivational vision changes from place to place, but it is usually an ever broadening group of contagious genuine followers of Jesus (thanks Mike Skelton, www.theinnerchange.org) who are growing and going into the world to accomplish the purpose. The visual image of that might be a huge wave, like the "pipeline."

12. Hock, *Birth of the Chaordic Age*, 8 (emphasis mine).

13. Ibid.

14. You may want to engage an outside coach to help you gain clarity on these crucial aspects. A weekend of exploration can move a congregation from confusion to clarity, from despair to passion. I have had the joy of leading many congregations on this journey. What an exciting thing to watch sleepy, bored eyes come to life as they are gripped with a passion for transformation.

15. Wayne Cordeiro, *Doing Church As a Team* (Ventura, Calif.: Gospel Light Publications, 2001).

16. "Chaordic: 1. the behavior of any self-governing organism, organization or system which harmoniously blends characteristics of order and chaos. 2. patterned in a way dominated by neither chaos or order." (Hock, *Birth of the Chaordic Age*, inside front cover).

17. Cesar Castellanos, *Successful Leadership through the Government of 12* (Bogota, Colombia: Editorial Vilit & Cia. Ltda., 1999), 210.

18. Dan Kimball, *The Emerging Church* (Grand Rapids, Mich.: Zondervan, 2003).

19. Fractaling is a concept used by Wayne Cordeiro. See Bill Easum, *Leadership on the Other Side* (Nashville: Abingdon Press, 2002) for an exercise on fractaling.

20. Jami Smith, Teaching Seminar (Lewisburg, Pennsylvania, 2003). Also see Integrity Music for Jami Smith's CDs.

21. Matt Redman, "Seeing You," Sparrow Records, 2004.

22. Some questions I ask people who want to be worship leaders are:
- Tell me/us about your personal worship experiences.
- Tell me/us about your life. Have you known joy? sorrow? pain? How have you dealt with that?
- Tell me/us what you listen to at home. What is your current favorite worship song that leads you into God's presence? Are there any "secular songs" that have led you into God's presence?
- Tell me/us about your musical gifts.
- Tell me/us about your experience with choirs, bands, professional musicians, and nonpaid musicians.
- Have you ever formed a band from scratch?
- What are you reading?
- What types of music are you playing?
- What is your experience leading worship?
- What is your experience with PowerPoint or presentation software?
- What is your experience with sound production?
- What do you know about "the Emerging Church"?
- What is your personal mission statement?
- Do you have any questions you want to ask me?

Before I would hire anyone I would want to have them read the congregation's Purpose and Principle statements, and I would want to know if they could "own and live by" these concepts.

23. *A Prairie Home Companion* with Garrison Keillor has been per-

forming tremendous drama for years. Many of their ideas would work well in a church situation.

24. See www.midnightoilproductions.com. Len Wilson and Jason Moore have developed the premier business in Christian-related multimedia development.

25. See www.bayareafellowship.com. They usually have original clips in worship.

26. Proverbs 7:23: "little knowing it will cost him his life" (NIV).

27. Eric Haines, Digital Media Specialist, Williamsport, Pennsylvania. Contact Eric at ericjhaines1@suscom.net.

28. Names are changed.

4. Tactical Steps for the Divine Intersection

1. Tom Bandy, live presentation (Houston, 2003).

2. Terry Teykl, *How to Pray after You Have Kicked the Dog* (Muncie, Ind.: Prayer Point Press, 1999), 203-307.

3. From his poem "Washington Monument by Night."

4. T. E. Lawrence, *Seven Pillars of Wisdom: A Triumph* (New York: Anchor, 1991), 9.

5. David Loar, e-mail message to author, April 2005.

6. An older woman came to me following an Easter Sunday service that celebrated the joy of Christ's resurrection and how that means we, too, can have life (1 Corinthians 15). She said she had a question. Seems her last pastor told her you can't ever know God and can't ever know for sure if you will go to heaven. He told her, "All you can do is hope you die on a day when God is in a good mood." She wondered who was right, me or this other pastor.

7. By the time you have defined *Pharisee, Sadducee*, and *Essene*, most of the congregation no longer cares. What works in a classroom often will not work in a Sunday service.

8. Special thanks to Dr. Robert Jacks for the hours teaching me to read aloud. Few schools have a department dedicated to the delivery of the message as profound as Princeton's.

9. The use of video is crucial in both presentation issues and delivery content. Compare your delivery with the high-impact, fast pace of MTV or with Robert Schuller. If you had two television sets in the room, one with you and your message and one with MTV, which one would eighteen- to twenty-five-year-olds watch? Who is speaking their language best?

10. Dee Hock, *Birth of the Chaordic Age* (San Francisco: Berrett-Koehler Publishers, 1999), 146. Hock outlines the need for every thriving organization to be an organism. Each thriving organism has three components: heaven (purpose, principles, and people), purgatory (structure and organization), and hell (rules and regulations). You want to spend as much time in heaven as you can, make only brief visits to purgatory, and avoid hell if you can.

11. Most denominations labor under guidelines established at least two hundred years ago. These rule books (Hock's hell, see n. 9) continue to stifle and hinder growth. I believe it is time for a new organizational structure. See my book *If It Can Happen Here* (Nashville: Abingdon Press, 2002) for a brief description of a new model.

12. Pastors in this denomination are "appointed" at the discretion of the bishop and supervising elders (district superintendents). I think that in this new age some of the major lessons for mainline denominations are: Long pastorates are essential. Allow thriving congregations to plant new churches—conferences have a mixed record of this, most do it poorly. Don't fix what isn't broken. If the congregation is reaching people for Jesus Christ and the pastor and the congregation are against a move, it should be *impossible* for a Bishop to move a pastor/leader from that appointment.

13. Dan Lentz's Web site, www.smallgroups.com, is a terrific resource for your small group.

14. Each article in the worship center was carried out of the room as the room was made increasingly dark. There was the clashing of the cymbal and the total darkness at the end of the process. This was followed by a small spotlight centered on a cross with a crown of thorns on the top and a black cloth around the juncture of the wooden beams.

15. Dr. Craig Cramer is Professor of Organ at Notre Dame University. You can purchase his recordings by searching www.amazon.com for his name or you can order directly from him at ccramer@nd.edu.

16. i-Worship is from Integrity Music, Mobile, Alabama, 1-800-239-7000.

17. *Worship Leader Magazine*, 26311 Junipero Serra, Suite 130, San Juan Capistrano, California 92675-1633, or www.worshipleader.com.

18. *Song DISCovery* is available at the same address as *Worship Leader* or at www.songdiscovery.com.

19. Hosanna! Music, *Experience Worship*, 2003 Integrity Media, Inc., Mobile, Alabama. www.integritymusic.com/worship/index.html?target=links/body.html.

20. *Vision Magazine*, P.O. Box 722786, Norman, Oklahoma 73070, or www.visionondemand.net.

21. Christian Copyright License International (CCLI) can be reached by calling 1-800-234-2446 or visiting their Web site at www.ccli.com.

5. Possible Pitfalls

1. George Fox was the founder of the Quakers and had many dynamic experiences with God.

2. The Pastoral Counselor in me must also offer caution here. I have seen young men and women who have literally cut a hand off or tried to pluck an eye out. Our experiences with God ought to lead to greater health, not destruction of our lives and bodies in what can only be described as a demented and tormented expression of a troubled soul.

3. These people, most likely unknown to you, have literally given it all for the sake of the gospel, leaving comfort and security for the uncertain future of developing new congregations and ministries in the United States.

4. Thomas G. Bandy, *Fragile Hope* (Nashville: Abingdon Press, 2002), from the cover.

5. James H. Charlesworth, "The Historical Jesus and Exegetical Theology," *The Princeton Seminary Bulletin* 22, no. 1 (2001): 46-63. Some of what Charlesworth writes is essential (pp. 49-50):

> Jesus grew up in Nazareth.
> He was baptized by John the Baptizer.
> He was obsessed with doing God's will.
> He was "intoxicated" with another dimension, and identified himself as a prophet.
> He chose twelve men to be his disciples.
> He was very close with Mary Magdalene.
> He performed healing miracles.
> He taught in synagogues (at the beginning only, perhaps), small dwellings, and on the fringes of villages (not cities).
> In shocking contrast to many Pharisees and the Essenes, he associated with the outcast, physically sick or impaired, and social misfits.
> He went to Jerusalem to celebrate Passover and worship within the temple cult.
> He frequented the temple, worshipped there, and taught in the porticoes.

When he was in Jerusalem he attacked some corruptions in the temple cult.

His meals were often religious events, and his last meal with his disciples was at Passover time in Jerusalem.

He seems to have been betrayed by Judas and was certainly denied by Peter.

He was forcefully taken by some Jews, most likely some related to the cult.

He was crucified by Roman soldiers outside the western walls of Jerusalem.

He died before the beginning of the Sabbath on Friday afternoon.

6. Ibid., 60.

Epilogue

1. Christina G. Rossetti, "The Bleak Midwinter," *The United Methodist Hymnal* (Nashville: The United Methodist Publishing House, 1989), 221.

A Brief Experiment in Divine Intersection

1. To access this iMix you must first download the iTunes software at www.apple.com/itunes/download/. Once you have this software installed go to the iTunes music store. At the music store you will see the iMix tab on the left side of the screen; click on it. Once at the iMix screen you can search for various playlists. In the search window type in "God at Crossroads." In the next pull down list, make sure you are searching for iMix name. Then hit the search button. My playlist will appear. Click on it, download the songs, and you will have all you need.

BIBLIOGRAPHY

Bandy, Thomas G. *Christian Chaos: Revolutionizing the Congregation.* Nashville: Abingdon Press, 1999.

———. *Coaching Change.* Nashville: Abingdon Press, 2000.

———. *Fragile Hope.* Nashville, Abingdon Press, 2002.

———. *Kicking Habits: Welcome Relief for Addicted Churches.* Nashville: Abingdon Press, 1997.

———. *Mission Mover.* Nashville: Abingdon Press, 2004.

———. *Moving Off the Map: A Field Guide to Changing the Congregation.* Nashville: Abingdon Press, 1998.

———. *Road Runner.* Nashville: Abingdon Press, 2002.

Barna, George. *The Barna Report.* Ventura, Calif.: The Barna Research Group, published quarterly through fall of 1999.

———. *User Friendly Churches.* Ventura, Calif.: Regal Books, 1991.

Benedict, Daniel T., and Craig Kennet Miller. *Contemporary Worship for the 21st Century: Worship or Evangelism?* Nashville: Discipleship Resources, 1994.

Burke, Spencer, and Colleen Pepper. *Making Sense of Church.* El Cajon, Calif.: Zondervan, 2003.

Castellanos, Cesar. *Dream and You Will Win the World!* Bogota, Colombia: Editorial Vilit & Cia. Ltd., 2002.

———. *Successful Leadership through the Government of 12.* Bogota, Colombia: Editorial Vilit & Cia. Ltd., 2002.

Charlesworth, James H. "The Historical Jesus and Exegetical Theology." *The Princeton Seminary Bulletin* 22, no. 1 (2001): 46-63.

Cordeiro, Wayne. *Doing Church As a Team*. Ventura, Calif.: Gospel Light Publications, 2001.

Dobson, Ed. *Starting a Seeker Sensitive Service: How Traditional Churches Can Reach the Unchurched*. Grand Rapids, Mich.: Zondervan, 1993.

Easum, William M. *Church Growth Handbook: Includes Complete Ministry Audit*. Nashville: Abingdon Press, 1990.

———. *The Complete Ministry Audit: How to Measure Twenty Principles for Growth*. Nashville: Abingdon Press, 1996.

———. *Dancing with Dinosaurs: Ministry in a Hostile and Hurting World*. Nashville: Abingdon Press, 1993.

———. *Leadership on the OtherSide: No Rules, Just Clues*. Nashville: Abingdon Press, 2000.

———. *Living in Faith Everyday: A Workbook for L.I.F.E. Groups*. Port Aransas, Tex.: William Easum, 1992.

———. *Sacred Cows Make Gourmet Burgers: Ministry Anytime, Anywhere by Anybody*. Nashville: Abingdon Press, 1995.

Easum, William M., and Thomas G. Bandy. *Growing Spiritual Redwoods*. Nashville: Abingdon Press, 1997.

Easum, Bill, and Dave Travis. *Beyond the Box: Innovative Churches That Work*. Loveland, Colo.: Group Publishing, 2003.

Friedman, Edwin H. *Generation to Generation: Family Process in Church and Synagogue*. New York: Guilford Press, 1985.

Galloway, Dale. *20/20 Vision: How to Create a Successful Church with Lay Pastors and Cell Groups*. Portland: Scott Publishing, 1986.

Hawkins, Thomas R. *Building God's People: A Workbook for Empowering Servant Leaders*. Nashville: Discipleship Resources, 1990.

Hock, Dee. *Birth of the Chaordic Age*. San Francisco: Berrett-Koehler Publishers, 1999.

Hunter, George G., III. *Church for the Unchurched*. Nashville: Abingdon Press, 1996.

———. *How to Reach Secular People*. Nashville: Abingdon Press, 1992.

Hybels, Lynne, and Bill Hybels. *Rediscovering Church: The Story and Vision of Willow Creek Community Church*. Grand Rapids, Mich.: Zondervan, 1995.

Kallestad, Walt. *Entertainment Evangelism: Taking the Church Public*. Nashville: Abingdon Press, 1996.

Kallestad, Walt, and Steven L. Schey. *Total Quality Ministry.* Minneapolis: Augsburg Press, 1994.

Kimball, Dan. *The Emerging Church.* Grand Rapids, Mich.: Zondervan, 2003.

————. *Emerging Worship.* Grand Rapids, Mich.: Zondervan, 2004.

Lewis, C. S. *A Grief Observed.* New York: Seabury Press, 1961.

————. *The Lion, the Witch and the Wardrobe. The Tales of Narnia.* New York: Collier Books, 1950.

Lewis, Phillip V. *Transformational Leadership: A New Model for Total Church Involvement.* Nashville: Broadman & Holman, 1996.

Loder, James E. *The Transforming Moment: Understanding Convictional Experiences.* San Francisco: Harper & Row, 1981.

Lucado, Max. *No Wonder They Call Him the Savior.* Portland: Multnomah Press, 1986.

Mallory, Sue. *The Equipping Church.* Grand Rapids, Mich.: Zondervan, 2001.

McLaren, Brian D. *The Church on the Other Side.* Grand Rapids, Mich.: Zondervan, 2000.

————. *A New Kind of Christian.* San Francisco: Jossey-Bass, 2001.

————. *The Story We Find Ourselves In.* San Francisco: Jossey-Bass, 2003.

Mead, Loren B. *The Once and Future Church: Reinventing the Congregation for a New Mission Frontier.* Bethesda, Md.: Alban Institute, 1991.

————. *Transforming Congregations for the Future.* Bethesda, Md.: Alban Institute, 1994.

Miller, Craig Kennet. *Baby Boomer Spirituality.* Nashville: Discipleship Resources, 1992.

Miller, Kim. *Handbook for Multi-Sensory Worship.* Nashville: Abingdon Press, 1999.

Morgenthaler, Sally. *Worship Evangelism.* Grand Rapids, Mich.: Zondervan, 1999.

Navarro, Kevin J. *The Complete Worship Leader.* Grand Rapids, Mich.: Baker Books, 2002.

Nixon, Paul. *Fling Open the Doors.* Nashville: Abingdon Press, 2002.

Park, Andy. *To Know You More.* Downers Grove, Ill.: InterVarsity Press, 2002.

Patton, Jeff. *If It Could Happen Here . . .* Nashville: Abingdon Press, 2002.

Redman, Matt. *The Unquenchable Worshipper.* Ventura, Calif.: Regal Books, 2001.

Rutz, James H. *The Open Church.* Auburn, Maine: SeedSowers, 1992.

Sample, Tex. *Hard Living People and Mainstream Christians.* Nashville: Abingdon Press, 1993.

———. *The Spectacle of Worship in a Wired World: Electronic Culture and the Gathered People of God.* Nashville: Abingdon Press, 1998.

———. *White Soul: Country Music, the Church, and Working People.* Nashville: Abingdon Press, 1996.

Scott, Dan. *The Emerging American Church.* Anderson, Ind.: Bristol Books, 1993.

Shorter Catechism of the Westminster Assembly. Published for the General Assembly by the Program Agency of the United Presbyterian Church in the United States of America.

Slaughter, Michael. *Out on the Edge: A Wake-up Call for Church Leaders on the Edge of the Media Reformation.* Nashville: Abingdon Press, 1998.

———. *Spiritual Entrepreneurs: Six Principles for Risking Renewal.* Nashville: Abingdon Press, 1995.

Sweet, Leonard. *Aqua Church.* Loveland, Colo.: Group Publishing, 1999.

———. *Soul Tsunami: Sink or Swim in New Millennium Culture.* Grand Rapids, Mich.: Zondervan, 1999.

Teykl, Terry. *Blueprint for the House of Prayer.* Muncie, Ind.: Prayer Point Press, 1996.

———. *How to Pray After You Have Kicked the Dog.* Muncie, Ind.: Prayer Point Press, 1999.

———. *Pray the Price.* Muncie, Ind.: Prayer Point Press, 1997.

———. *The Presence Based Church.* Muncie, Ind.: Prayer Point Press, 2003.

———. *Your Pastor: Preyed on or Prayed For.* Anderson, Ind.: Bristol Books, 1994.

Warren, Rick. *The Purpose Driven Church: Growth without Compromising Your Message and Mission.* Grand Rapids, Mich.: Zondervan, 1995.

Wills, Dick. *Waking to God's Dream: Spiritual Leadership and Church Renewal.* Nashville: Abingdon Press, 1999.

Wilson, Len. *The Wired Church: Making Media Ministry.* Nashville: Abingdon Press, 1999.

Wright, Timothy. *A Community of Joy: How to Create Contemporary Worship.* Nashville: Abingdon Press, 1994.

Wright, Tim, and Jan Wright, eds. *Contemporary Worship: A Sourcebook for Spirited-Traditional, Praise and Seeker Services.* Nashville: Abingdon Press, 1997.

Yaconelli, Michael. *Messy Spirituality.* Grand Rapids, Mich.: Zondervan, 2002.

Yancey, Philip. *The Jesus I Never Knew.* Grand Rapids, Mich.: Zondervan, 1995.

Zschech, Darlene. *Extravagant Worship.* Minneapolis: Bethany House, 2002.

Discography

Audio Adrenaline. *Underdog*. Forefront Records. 1999.

Baloche, Paul. *God of Wonders*. Hosanna! Music. 2001.

———. *Open the Eyes of My Heart*. Hosanna! Music. 2000.

Barnett, Marie. *The Air I Breathe*. Mercy/Vineyard Publishing. 1995.

Breland, Jason. *Believe*. Hosanna! Music. 2003.

Cottrell, Travis. *Alive Forever*. Hosanna! Music. 2004.

———. *Unashamed Love*. Hosanna! Music. 2003.

Crowe, Jesse. *Falling Castles*. Just for the Record. 2001.

Delerious. *World Service*. Furious Music. 2003.

Doerksen, Brian. *Today*. Hosanna! Music. 2004.

Evanescence. *Fallen*. Wind-up Records. 2003.

Fitts, Bob. *I Will Bow to You*. Hosanna! Music. 2001.

Hope of the Nations. Hosanna! Music. 2003.

House of Worship. Integrity Music. 2002.

Krauss, Alison, and Union Station. *So Long So Wrong*. Rounder Records. 1997.

LeBlanc, Lenny. *Above All*. Hosanna! Music. 1999.

———. *One Desire*. Hosanna! Music. 2002.

Lubben, Dave. *A Place Called Surrender*. Vertical Music. 2003.

McPherson, Matt, and Sherry McPherson. *I Will Rejoice*. Worship Resources Kit. Autumn Records. 2000. www.autumnrecords.com.

MercyMe. *Almost There*. INO Records. 2001.

Neal, Michael. *Made Me Glad*. Hosanna! Music. 2004.

New Life Church, Colorado Springs. *More Than Life*. Hosanna! Music. 2002. Jared Anderson, worship leader.

Parsley, Ross. *I Am Free*. Hosanna! Music. 2004.

Passion: OneDay Live (DVD). Sparrow Records. 2000.

Redman, Matt. *Facedown*. Sparrow Records. 2004.

Rice, Chris. *Short Term Memories*. Rocketown Records. 2004.

Scott, Kathryn. *Satisfy*. Vertical Music. 2003.

Slaughter, Alvin. *Rain Down*. Hosanna! Music. 2000.

Smith, Jami. *Wash Over Me*. Hosanna! Music. 2002.

Smith, Michael W. *Worship*. Hosanna! Music. 2000.

Song DISCovery. Volume 43. Hosanna! Music. 2004.

Vertli, Danny. *Hymns and Prayers*. Hapi Skratch Records. 1999.

Walker, Tommy. *Make It Glorious*. Hosanna! Music. 2004.

Womack, Lee Ann. *I Hope You Dance*. MCA. 2000.

For other CDs you might like, check the artists listed below.
Big Daddy Weave
Brooklyn Tabernacle Choir
Chris Rice
Chris Tomlin
Cindy Foote
Darlene Zschech
David Crowder Band
Don Moen
Eoghan Heaslip
Jason Walls
Lakewood Church
Margaret Becker
Planetshakers
Tim Timmons